D0040494

Repetition

Repetition

Rebecca Reilly

Four Way Books

Tribeca

Copyright © 2015 Rebecca Reilly
No part of this book may be used or reproduced in any manner
without written permission except in the case of brief quotations embodied in critical
articles and reviews.

Please direct all inquiries to:
Editorial Office
Four Way Books
POB 535, Village Station
New York, NY 10014
www.fourwaybooks.com

Library of Congress Cataloging-in-Publication Data

Reilly, Rebecca, [date]
[Poems. Selections]
Repetition / Rebecca Reilly.
pages cm
ISBN 978-1-935536-58-1 (alk. paper)
I. Title.
PS3618.E564528R48 2015
811'.6--dc23
2014030219

This book is manufactured in the United States of America and printed on
acid-free paper.

Four Way Books is a not-for-profit literary press. We are grateful for the assistance
we receive from individual donors, public arts agencies, and private foundations.

This publication is made possible with public funds from the
New York State Council on the Arts, a state agency.

State of the Arts

NYSCA

[clmp]

We are a proud member of the Council of Literary Magazines and Presses.
Distributed by University Press of New England
One Court Street, Lebanon, NH 03766

Contents

Prologue

Why does reading Gertrude Stein make me happy? This question begins the investigation. I am trying to know something. Something I could not know before is coming up in my body. When it reached consciousness, it broke me. I will tell you about how that came to pass, as I am trying to know it myself. A book is a journey—we do not know what will come to pass. Sometimes the author knows in advance of us. Sometimes the author does not. These are the books I prefer. As Nietzsche wrote of his dear enemy Pascal:

One should not conceal and corrupt the facts of how our thoughts have come to us. The profoundest and least exhausted books will always have something of the aphoristic and unexpected character of Pascal's Pensées.

We should not conceal the order of our thoughts. I will not conceal from you the order of my thoughts; I will not conceal them from myself: until I am exhausted.

Why does reading Gertrude Stein make me happy? Why does almost everything else I do make me unhappy? I suspect the answer to both questions lies in repetition. I thought for a long time about the difference between good repetition and bad repetition.

Those who suffer belong only to God, wrote Nelly Sachs in a letter to Paul Celan. Those who suffer exist outside of time. Mental suffering is inexhaustible, and is thus pierced through with eternity.

Repetition
[*Le Monde Irréel*]

Paris is the city of my grief, one in which I was dead too, for exile is a kind of afterlife: unreal, emptied of time— another dimension where time has stopped.

Even the beauty of Paris lent itself to this sense of unreality, because like all beauty, it is complete and self-sufficient. Beauty doesn't need us. It empties the mind of thought.

The poet René Char wrote, *Dans nos ténèbres, il n'y a pas une place pour la beauté. Toute la place est pour la beauté.*

[In our shadows, there is not one place for beauty. The whole place is for beauty.]

The beauty of Paris is impermeable and impenetrable. Only the sky is a permeable membrane. In winter, the sky is silver and the air is misty, a vibrating tin, which matches the slate roofs. I would sit in the Jardin des Plantes and memorize the names of flowers and think nothing.

It was a lonely time, but a clear loneliness with no thoughts in it.

Eight months after my father died, I moved to Paris.
I could not speak, I could not feel, and I was alone.
My ghostly companions in the city of the dead were
Gertrude Stein and Paul Celan: my happy friend and my
sad friend. Celan was thus the more constant companion
in my grief, and accompanied me particularly in my
walks along the Seine, hunched and smoking in his long
grey overcoat as he hurried along the *quais.* Through
the arcades of the Palais-Royal, beneath the *Paulownias*
[Paul] of the Place de la Contrescarpe, in his quarter,
the bourgeois 15ème, to his building, 6 avenue Émile-
Zola, across from the Pont Mirabeau *sous lequel coule la
Seine,* and on the Pont Mirabeau to watch the Seine *coule*
and imagine jumping in. Did you face east toward your
home, or west, away from Paris?

On se promène. On se promène ensemble.

[We walk. We walk together.]

These are the places that belong to us, Paul Celan and I.
We most loved to sit in the Jardin des Plantes with the
sun on our faces, and watch the blowing clouds move
east over the pierced grey cupolas of the *musée* [the sky
was always billowing in the glass of the great windows of
the museum], over the aligned gardens, over the green
oxidized glass [which turned pink in east-light] and
blanched iron scaffold of the hothouses [*serres botaniques*].
We liked also to walk the orderly rows of the gardens and
write the names of plants in our notebooks:

*aster / marguerite-reine / aster de chine / fougère / chèvrefeuille /
muguet de mai / narcisse des poètes [selfishness] / pensée / pavot
coquelicot . . . /*

My favorite being the dahlias of September, their lion
heads like rust fire. Paul liked the *perce-neige* of February
[consolation].

Everything I saw I showed my father, who I pretended
to carry within me [*where I go, you go*], to comfort him,
so he would not be alone in his death. For his birthday,
we went to the zoo in the Jardin des Plantes [my father
grew up in the Bronx and loved the Bronx Zoo more
than almost anywhere]. The *flamants* of Rilke were there,
always and still, pink and perched on one leg, asleep with
their long necks folded into their bodies, but I did not see
his leopard. I too have wasted my life asleep.

We met an elderly man promenading in the *allées* as we
sat on a bench beneath the *châtaigners*. He wore a well-
cut tweed overcoat and a fine hat and walked with his
hands clasped behind his back, slightly hunched forward.
I don't know why he spoke to me. When he heard
my accent, he asked where I came from. I answered:
l'Amerique. Mais d'où? he asked. *Des États Unis. Mais, je suis
américain aussi—je viens d'Uruguay. Nous sommes tous les deux
américains, non?* He smiled. Yes, we are both Americans.

I thought often of Linnaeus in the garden—the precision of his descriptions. Once there was an exhibition of photos in the garden, accompanied by text from his *Systema Naturae*. The photographs were of flowers described in the book, blown up to about 3x3 feet. They were taken from so close to the surface of the flower as to be unbearably intimate—like a pink-shot of a vagina. Even the small cilia stood out on the surface of the flowers as one was *face à face* with their sexual organs. The text by Linnaeus was also pornographic in nature:

Plants with nine stamens and one pistil: *Nine men in the same bride's chamber, with one woman.*

It was like being dead, which was nice. I existed in
a beautiful afterlife, my mind evacuated by beauty.
One may disparage beauty, one may revile beauty,
and I admit that beauty and evil are two sides of the
same *feuille* [leaf / page]: both are perfect, complete in
themselves, and thus have no need of us.

Beauty is a closed metaphysical system enamored of
itself. As my friend Nietzsche wrote, *the only thing of beauty
in a failed system is the personal element.* A world constructed
to be known through the mind is a failure; a system
constructed to protect one from the world is a beautiful
machine which has not yet failed. You may know what is
coming for me—I do not yet.

The body of Paul Celan was found seven kilometers downstream in Courbevoie on May 1, 1970—the day I was born. It is thought he jumped from the Pont Mirabeau into the Seine on or about the evening of April 20, 1970. I do not know how these dates connect us, but they do. *Sous le pont Mirabeau coule la Seine*—a silty green river with swift currents. I cannot imagine choosing drowning. The body must fight against it, against your will to let your lungs fill and to sink down. All French schoolchildren must memorize this poem. Ask any French person and they will know at least this line: *Sous le pont Mirabeau coule la Seine.*

Later I could imagine it. Everything inside me broke.
Everything inside me was broken. I thought just go
home. If it doesn't get better, you can jump off one
of their large bridges. I rode my bicycle over the
Williamsburg Bridge, over the Manhattan Bridge—these
are not good for jumping. The Manhattan Bridge has
a chain-link fence and below the pedestrian walkway
of the Williamsburg runs only the road. The George
Washington Bridge is the best choice.

When I come out of therapy each Friday, I walk north, through Riverside Park, up through Washington Heights, twice, as far as Inwood, once, to the northern tip of the island itself, as though an explorer. On each walk I can see the George Washington Bridge, and it calms me to know I can jump off it if I need to. Nietzsche said that the thought of suicide is a comfort on many a sleepless night, and I know what he means. I know how death came and slept in your heart and was a comfort to you. Death whispers a promise: *I know the way out of here.*

Consider this small poem by Celan:

You were my death:
you I could hold,
when all fell from me.

When you have lost everything, when you are alone in
your depression, death is something you can hold onto.
The depressed person cannot remember ever feeling any
other way. Death is a door in this despair.

If we think of Celan's parents, their death was not their
own. Paul Celan lived in an afterlife, an exile, in excess
of his parents' death.

Exile is a suspension of time—a suspended sentence, to
be revoked later, without warning, at any moment, when
grief comes back for you.

I read an article about suicide on the Golden Gate
Bridge. One survivor of the fall who was interviewed
said, *As my hand left the rail I thought, I can fix everything in my
life but this.*

Andy came to visit me in Paris. I asked him—Do you
think that is why they survive—because they think that at
the last instant?

No, he said, they all think that.

We said goodbye on the railway platform at the airport.
In Paris, railway platforms are always inter-dimensional
spaces of transit, and I felt like he had come to visit from
the land of the living and was now returning.

He said, I love you, Rebecca.
I said, I don't know why anyone does.

I had to put my hand on my forehead to keep it from
breaking with grief—a gesture I was to repeat many
times in this period of my life.

Depression is not sorrow; it is the absence of feeling—to feel nothing.

The doctor asks, Do you feel as though you are encased in lead?

No—I am at the bottom of the ocean, and the weight of it presseth down upon me as much as impedeth forward motion.

I am at the bottom of the ocean and what passes above me is time. I am asleep beneath the enormous pressure of the water, and life continues above me, without me. This is a repetition I must get right. I must not fall asleep again.

Through repetition I am trying to know something. In French, repetition means to practice. A rehearsal for a play is *une répétition*. I am rehearsing for something; I am practicing very hard until I get it right. It will be perfect. [It is important that it not be perfect.]

In this afterlife, I moved invisibly among the living, but could not speak to them. This is a poetic way of saying: I could not speak French. It was difficult to communicate with those around me.

As in depression, each small task was weighted, slowed in gravity and time, and took the most careful preparation—to look up the word for "stamp," to learn the phrases which would enable you to buy one, to write down and practice speaking the phrases in order to be understood.

In my terrible grief this seemed adequate: the difficulty of my inner life was mirrored by the struggles of the outer one.

I had to learn everything over again—each thing I did was for the first time.

In this way I was a child: I had to learn to talk again, to feed and care for myself, to construct the most simple phrases, to learn the names of things anew.

My life had broken in two—the first part was over, and so it seemed natural to begin again in the new language, in the new country.

For the first time, my interior and exterior worlds were aligned in the precision and clarity of grief.

If I kept moving I could stay above it. If I kept running,
it could not pull me down into it. And so began the night
rides through Paris. I bought an old Dutch bike that I
loved more than anything I have ever owned [I love it
still], and began to ride through the streets at night
to make myself tired so I could sleep. I would ride for
miles—first to the Eiffel Tower and back along the *quais*
of the Seine. I would time the ride so as to arrive at the
Pont Neuf on the hour to watch the tower sparkle in
the distance [every hour on the hour], then continue
along the dark Seine to the tower itself, to stand below
it as it rained light like sparks [*étincelles*]. I felt so lucky
to be there with the light raining down on me. A tour
bus driver smoking by his bus said, *Pas mal, huh* and we
smiled at each other.

I had a *Plan de Paris*, and would mark the pages of my routes, a different colored pencil for each ride. In this way I could see which districts I had visited, and which remained to be explored. I am sure I have ridden on each street in Paris, though on many occasions was careless, did not mark the streets correctly, could not remember them accurately, or neglected to record the ride in its entirety. But I can visit these streets in my mind still when I close my eyes. If you name me a street in Paris, I can visit it in my eyes.

I liked to imagine living in the illuminated apartments I could see into from my bike. One particular street, the rue Linné, which passed behind the Jardin des Plantes, seemed to have many intellectuals—through the windows I saw walls of books. I thought: I will live here overlooking the garden with many books. I imagined the inhabitants must be professors at one of the nearby colleges, of which there were many. Once I found a great mirror, with leaded mercury glass, and carried it home. Joël said it must once have been mounted as part of a hearth. He could tell by the placement of the holes in the wood.

When I arrived in Paris, I was not sure it could ever become the interior city, displacing New York. For the first year, I would miss the clear open blue of the New York sky, the blindingly bright winter sun, the open vistas of the grid in which one is never lost. Over time though, I grew to love being lost in the circuitous rues, only to emerge on the long axis of a grand boulevard, the always hidden discoveries that awaited after each bend, if only one continued, went further. The center of gravity shifts, the city is displaced within, and the snowy globe fills with the façades of Paris.

It was always like that, this hidden life. If one just continued, something magic would happen. I was so lonely, but I would think: just go outside and see what happens. I rode over the Île Saint-Louis, over the Pont Louis-Philippe, around the bend of small rue de Brosse, past the Église Saint-Gervais, behind the Hôtel de Ville. Nuns in blue robes were entering with lit candles in paper. I locked my bike and followed them. It was the Feast of the Ascension and the choir of blue nuns sang, the candles lit the nave of the stone church, and the priest swung the thurible of incense. I am sure I was dead.

Chant final:

Nous avons vu la vraie lumière
Nous avons reçu l'Esprit celeste . . .

It was always like that, a fairytale in a forest in which the children are led onward by lights in the distance. Once I was riding my bike in the blueing dusk [*crépuscule*], through the Bois de Vincennes, among the darkening shadows of the trees over the dirt paths. In the distance I could see flickers of lights. As I came closer, it was an old wooden carousel, a common enough sight in the gardens of Paris, but through the falling night it seemed a mirage as the lights sparkled and turned and the music was very clear with no sounds around it in the darkness of the empty park.

You will not believe me, but there are four such apparitions in the Bois de Vincennes, and I could see each in the distance through the trees, and as I rode towards one, another would beckon me on. It was always like that, led on through the night from one miraculous event to another until finally you did not know how far you had come and could not return the way you had come.

You exited the park in an unknown quarter of the city, yet knowing in which direction to head [I have a good sense of direction and can usually tell which way is east, west, north, south—in Paris I knew by the light tilting west].

It was always like that, in Berlin, in the Tiergarten, walking along the Landwehr canal [which belongs to Paul Celan] past the zoo in the dark, the animals calling [the wolves howling!] in the dark across the canal, slow shadows moving behind the chain-link fence of the aviary, along the frozen path through the immense trees, to emerge in a forest of lanterns. Truly: a museum of lanterns, their gas lights flickering along the path.

A collection of lanterns from around Germany and the world: the candelabras of Paris, Art Deco from Dublin, many casts and styles from the burgs of Germany, even a lantern made of concrete etc. etc. etc. and you were led on and continued.

[Spandau, Leipzig, Dresden, Freiburg, Heidelberg, Wuppertal, Augsburg, Baden-Baden, Budapest, Zurich, Brugge, Charlottenburger Kandelaber, Pariser Strasse . . .]

Through the illuminated glass mantle you could see the small clicking mechanisms, like the inside of a clock, which powered the gas works—the sound the only one in the park around you.

Also behind the Jardin des Plantes was the Grand Mosque of Paris: a beautiful white mosque with shaded interior gardens where one could have a mint tea. I liked better the storefront mosques of my quarter, the recorded call of the muezzin over a scratchy loudspeaker, and the men in white robes, with round white caps, so many they could not fit within the small shop and so filled the street, which was closed to traffic [much to the chagrin of the French], hunched on their prayer rugs: rows of white human hillocks, in the pose of submission, facing toward Mecca.

I loved the month of Ramadan, the quiet streets asleep all day, then filling with bearded men in robes and caps waiting in long lines at the North African bakeries to buy *sucrée* honey pastries for the breaking of the fast. The restaurants full of families, the older women in burqas, the young often with colorful head scarves, but otherwise in the clothes typical of a French person of their age.

I loved living among Muslims, who were kinder to me than French people, knowing as they did what it is to be a stranger.

The two gentlemen, brothers, who owned the *épicerie*
at the bottom of my building, always smiled at me and
waved when I came home. They worked six days a week,
7 AM until *minuit*, closed on Mondays, just the two of
them, and lived on the first floor above the shop. They
alternated shifts: one slept in the day and worked in the
night, one the inverse. The shutters of their apartment
were always closed because one was always sleeping. On
Mondays, they cooked big meals which I could smell
passing on the stairs: tagines and couscous and often the
metallic smell of sardines roasting in their skin. Once they
closed for two weeks to go to Algeria because their father
had died. The French call them: *les Arabes du coin* [the Arabs
on the corner], as most *épiceries* [like a deli here] are owned
by North Africans, who are not, in fact, Arabs.

I visited Gertrude Stein a couple of times in Père Lachaise when I first arrived, and would think of her when riding past the cemetery on my bike—I did not live far from there. I left a rock on her grave and asked her to help me with my dissertation.

The first two months I took classes at the Alliance Française, just around the corner from Stein's house at 27 rue de Fleurus, and I would pass by there every day. You can peek through the grille of the gates into the courtyard where her apartment was.

Once, there were workmen painting the hallway and they let me in to look. The courtyard has a round garden at the center with flowers and large urns and ivy. What I guessed to be her apartment was just behind it, with the large industrial atelier windows common to courtyards in Montparnasse. I did not peek through the windows. Not from fear, I did not think of it at the time.

I thought most about Gertrude Stein in the Luxembourg Gardens, which are three blocks from her house, and imagined her promenading there with Alice and Basket. I thought of her when sitting in the two side gardens, which I called the secret gardens, hidden on the west side of the park, on either side of the entrance closest to her home. Both are tucked away from the geometrical grandeur and *allées* of the larger garden, and are like circular bowers, enclosed by trees, which mirror each other.

Each has a circle of lawn, fenced off with small metal arches, ankle high, and surrounded by a dirt path upon which were placed green metal chairs. In the center of the each circle was a statue, and around the statue was a spectacular display of flowers which rotated, as all the flowerbeds of Paris do, by season. It looked as though the statues were floating in a circle of flowers.

The flowers are arranged with great artistry, and I remember one display particularly—tall pink flowers on green stalks, interspersed with a series of graduating flowers of alternating heights and hues of pink and lavender. All of the flowerbeds of Paris are arranged in this way: a composition of flowers, with attention to each note and tone.

The chairs rotated around the circle according to where the sun was in the sky, as the French took their lunch in the park, and moved the chairs so as to take the sun on their faces.

Paris is arranged on a series of axes: an alignment of monuments and vistas which extend along Haussmann's boulevards, and draw the eye into the distance. If you stand before the pyramid in front of the Louvre, you can see in a straight line through the Tuileries, along the Champs-Élysées, to the Arc de Triomphe. If you were able to see further, you would see the Grande Arche de la Défense, which echoes the Arc de Triomphe, and lies slightly out of line from it, bending the axis a few degrees to the west.

If you exit the gardens from the rear gate and turn around, you are aligned with the Luxembourg Palace, and Sacré-Cœur is slightly to the left on the hill in the distance to the north.

If you turn and leave the park, the axis continues south, through a long alley of *châtaigniers*, their leaves and branches trimmed by men on cherry-pickers so as to be perfectly rectangular, to the Observatoire de Paris.

At the end of this *allée*, lies the Fontaine de l'Observatoire. In the center of the fountain, a column of four women hold a celestial sphere, which echoes the dome of the observatory behind it. Great horses with merman tails rear up from the waves below the women, and the marble basin is ringed by turtles, which face back toward the fountain, as water shoots from their mouths.

The women, the sphere, the horses, the fish, and the turtles are an oxidized green copper, and the women hold the sphere aloft so that from certain angles it rises directly before the dome of the observatory—a small moon and its planet.

One of the winters, the water of the fountain froze, as though time had stopped—jets of frozen water arced from the mouths of each turtle.

I was not alive, but I loved these places. Simone Weil lived just behind the gardens, and a plaque commemorates her residence on the rue Auguste-Comte.

I would choose any green patch [indicating a park] on the *Plan de Paris* and set off for it on my bicycle. In this way I found the chateau of the Bois de Boulogne. There are two kinds of roses: those of June, and the late ones of September. In the garden of the chateau, in the lower golden sun of September, I am sure the late roses were more dense and pendulous in their fragrance. I lay on the lawn next to the rose garden, hands entwined behind my head, and imagined I was Rilke.

When Napoleon was exiled in London, he admired the
English style of garden [a faux-naturalism such as one
may see in Central and Prospect Parks], as opposed
to the severe alignment of the French garden. He
commanded Parc Montsouris, on the southern edge
of Paris, and the Buttes-Chaumont in the far north, to
be constructed along the English model. The Buttes-
Chaumont was built upon the site of a former quarry,
on a steep incline, and the view from the park over the
city extends into the far eastern suburbs, white and
uniform in the distance. *Mont* and *butte*: both are words
for mountains. Paris is a river-valley, a basin which falls
and rises between these heights—so that rain clouds and
weather are often caught above it.

The quarter behind the Buttes-Chaumont looks as though a provincial village was left on a hilltop above Paris. Small alleys, called *villas*, transect the hill—terraced like a vineyard.

The narrow lanes are bordered by stone walls, overgrown with ivy and wisteria [by season: mimosa, roses, orange trumpet vines], which conceal small, private homes and gardens.

I discovered this quarter by chance, in search of rue Francis Ponge, which I had seen in the *Plan de Paris* and thus set out for on my bike. There was an African street fair on the rue Francis Ponge that day, with music and food and many Africans in their bright robes—the women with matching scarves wound high about their heads.

At night, I often stood on the Pont Sully and watched the *bateaux-mouches* roll shadows across the elegant houses of the Île Saint-Louis. The klieg lights of the boats cast shadows of the laurel trees along the *quai* onto the ochre facades.

The shadows rotated as though projected by car headlights, and, on the laurels themselves, the underside of each leaf was illuminated: a shining emerald when the leaves were green, glowing amber in fall. The lights of the boat moved below them, so each leaf was lit from below like a singular, transparent jewel.

The river at night was black, with sharp icy white stars broken across its surface. I used to call it the river of diamonds.

When we were children, my father drove us each weekend to my grandmother's house in the Bronx for Sunday dinner. As we drove over the George Washington Bridge, my father used to sing a song [which we thought he made up], and it went like this: George Washington Bridge, the George Washington Washington Bridge . . . that was it, those were the words, and you could sing them over and over again. The other joke he liked to tell, that we did not understand at the time, was this: Why is the lower level of the bridge called the Martha Washington? Punchline: because it lay under George.

I have a weird memory of riding over the bridge when it is announced on the radio that Elvis Presley has died.

Many years later I would go with my father on Saturdays
to visit my grandmother in the Alzheimer's ward of
St. Joseph's Hospital in Yonkers. She would be waiting
on a bench in front of the nurse's station, in a row with
other ladies, all holding their purses. The nurses called it
the bus stop.

My grandmother was allowed to keep her purse, but it
was empty. She would ask us again and again, Now who
are you? My father was good at making her laugh, and
getting her off the repetitive question track. He would
say, Do you know how old you are? She would say, No!

He would say: You   are   *ninety-five*   years   old!

Oh! she would say—throwing her hands up in surprise
and laughing, You can't kill a bad thing.

He would ask her again: Do you know how old you are?
She would give the same answer. It was like a routine.
It was funny each time.

At the end of the visit, he would say, We're going down
to the store to get some things for dinner. She'd say, Let
me give you some money—I'll roast a chicken and make
potatoes and carrots. He'd say, You can give me the
money when we get back. Then we would go.

What she could remember, was her childhood in Ireland,
and my father would ask her to sing the songs she had
learnt in school there and she would.

This time in New York, I've been twice to his childhood home in the Bronx. I had not been there since the late 1970s—I think my grandmother moved to Bronxville in 1978—but I could remember where it was, how to get there, and what it looked like.

I got off the subway at Dyckman, crossed the Harlem River over a small peaked steel bridge, and walked around and up the hill, past a row of garages and chop shops, to Andrews Avenue. At the foot of the street is St. Nicholas of Tolentine, where my father went to grammar and high school, and further up the hill is University Heights—the bluffs overlooking the Harlem River, where Bronx Borough Community College is now, on the site of the former northern campus of NYU.

I went the day after my aunt died, a hot, humid day in May, and the men sitting on cars outside the bodega, and on the stoop of my father's building, looked at me with mild interest, acknowledging that I was a stranger, but with neither menace nor welcome. I wondered if I should tell them that my father had lived here, but it seemed too eager.

I think I knew which building it was, though as with all childhood memories, it was much smaller now. What I had remembered as a large courtyard with terraced steps, where we used to play, was still there, exactly the same, but smaller and more narrow.

The feeling of looking down from a great height, through time, into a mythical place, which exists, not merely in memory—that one could actually go there—was slightly hallucinatory. Time wavered, as though I might see him playing on the steps with his friends, aged seven or eight.

The second time I went up there was on the anniversary
of his death. I walked up Andrews Avenue, past his
building, past the Art Deco facades, the now grimy
tile friezes and lintels, marble balustrades, past the
abandoned, boarded-up houses, the bright red and
yellow house of the Buddhist temple, up to the bluffs
overlooking the Harlem river, across to Washington
Heights and Inwood, along the bend in the river to
Spuyten Duyvil, to the Hudson beyond. I needed a new
perspective, to climb up out of the city. This time in New
York, the temporary one, I need to go back into the deep
past, past the time I lived here before, into something
deeper—farther in the past and farther down in me.

The day before my father's birthday, I saw a *rouge gorge* [red throat] singing in a berry tree in an *allée* of Parc André Citroën. I was sure it was him. This is my least favorite park in Paris, with its severe terraces and angles, but I gave English lessons to the CFO of a bank next to it, so would eat my lunch there sometimes. I can't remember his name [Monsieur Escaléra], but he used to sit very close next to me at the table, and sometimes would show me pictures of his vacation house in Provence. Once when the lesson was over he said, You don't have to go. I said that I had another appointment. During the week his secretary called the school and requested another teacher [I got in trouble].

Later, I would imagine being his mistress and being kept in a nice apartment. I am a slow reactor to events.

I went to see the Walton Ford show at the Hamburger
Bahnhof. I liked to ride my bike there, along the canal,
past the watchtower, and through the graveyard which
formed part of the no man's land that once lay along
the wall. Berlin is a city of liminal spaces, *terrain vague /
vague terrain*. I bought you a postcard there and wrote
a José Martí poem on it [the text of which had been
included by Ford in the painting]:

I wish to leave the world
By its natural door
In my tomb of green leaves
They are to carry me to die.
Do not put me in the dark
To die like a traitor;
I am good, and like a good thing
I will die with my face in the sun.

It was one of the happiest days of my life. Don't be sad
if I say it was the happiest. I was so in love with you,
everyone could see it on my face. Men, strangers, would
come up and speak to me [quite unusual in Germany].
I rode my bike to the museum, I bought you that card, I
rode to Humboldthain pool [another favorite place] and
swam, I went to the studio and wrote the poem on the
card for you.

This was a different day, but looking out the bright
industrial windows at the park, the sun shining, the
birds singing in the trees [really!], the long whine of the
S-bahn pulling away from Humboldthain through the
trees, I thought: you are just you now.

A walk around the block revealed things that I had
thought were far were in fact near: the canal, the ateliers
and graffiti, the Turkish social club with the meringue
ceiling, like an Ottoman palace, the old Turkish men, in
jackets, drinking tea from small glasses at tables set out
along the canal.

All the externals and expectations that compass a life—
family, country, language—had fallen away and I was free.

Take everything away and what you are left with is you.
You are just you. I touched it only that one time.

I would go work at Darrell's studio while he was away in San Francisco—mostly pretend I was going to write my dissertation, read a few pages of *Repetition*, look out the wall of windows at the park, into the kitchens of the Turkish women across the courtyard, take naps on the day bed.

Sometimes I would have tea in the kitchen with the Italian artist up the hall—she painted most days, all day, and would show me her giant canvases from time to time. She would say, You and I, we are workers—we arrive every day for work. I hadn't written a poem in years.

I returned here to know where I lost you. I had not meant to.

I could not stop losing things: *I lost two cities, lovely ones. And, vaster . . .* I began to be astonished at myself, to regard myself as though a stranger—as I continued to lose, farther and faster.

When you left, something I had built against my whole life began to break. I could not fix it anymore.

You were the last thing I needed to lose.

I ran for so long and when I stopped running it caught me. What I owed came due.

The first grief returned with a swift blow that took me down.

I asked to break open. What did I know of breaking, of being broken? I cried like a child, I want to go home I want to go home, but there is no home to go back to.

December: I went back. New York was brutal and insane. I could not believe how dirty it was, how loud, the piles of garbage, the rats and how sad the people are.

I rented an apartment in Bed-Stuy for a while. Even the supermarket seemed hallucinogenic—all the unnatural colors and no actual food.

Not long before my father died, my sister tried to kill herself again. I said to my father, I'm not helping anymore I'm not coming. He started to cry. I'd never seen him cry before. I said, You are like a bag of rats who are drowning and clawing each other to death as you drown. I'm not coming with you.

In this way, New York is like my family, and is my home: insane, loud, narcissistic, invasive, without boundaries, full of aggression, ambient rage and despair. The mentally ill and the narcissists who are also mentally ill shouting into their phones, led through the streets by the blue screens of their devices. Go in the street and look at the faces of the next ten people you see. Is one of them happy?

New York is an addiction. No matter how desperate and hunted you are, you think you need it. Then you quit, you leave, and everything is much quieter. You think, Oh, it is perfectly fine here [in the new place].

Later, before I moved back to New York, I could not find the card. I kept thinking I'd find it and mail it to you. It would be an excuse to contact you again. Now it is just one the lost things I dream of: a small, blue-lacquered Chinese bowl [*I sneak in to my old house to find it and have to hide from the new owners*], my apartment in Paris, my books, you [*we are in a dark house and you won't look at me—I have to go out and am afraid you will leave while I am gone—I am lost in a German city (Leipzig?) on my bicycle and can't get back to you—a boy I know from my hometown says he can lead me home, but he rides too fast and I am lost again*].

According to Lacan, behind the dream lies the real.

I look for you in the dream and behind the dream.

The real, he tells us, is something encountered in a space which opens up once returning [repetition] is *no longer* the way in which something comes back to the subject. The italics [his] are ominous augurs.

I will tell you later of the real that tore open once I refused a repetition.

Anton dreams he is in a field, at the edge of a cliff. Trees are falling from the sky and he has to catch them. They look like Christmas trees and they keep falling but he can't catch them all.

Riding the bike so much changed the shape of my body. My calves and hips and ass became muscular. I fucked Anton again the first summer I came home to visit. I was moving up and down on his cock and he said, Oh, your hips are different, as he held them.

We walked through Williamsburg to Greenpoint, along
Driggs, through McCarren Park, stopping to visit the
Cathedral of Transfiguration. I used to love the verdigris
domes—I lived beside them for so long. I wanted to see
it again, to take it back to Paris with me, to describe it
correctly. The interior dome a sky of tempera blue—
constellations embedded in gold inlay.

Anaximander imagined stars fixed on a crystalline
sphere, rotating around the earth.

I walked with him through Monsignor McGolrick Park—a very Parisian type of square, but with great elms along the linear alleys, and Polish men drinking vodka on the benches. As I described my life in Paris to him, he said—Oh, you're happy. This caught me, as I had never thought of being happy before. In the center of the park, which I had passed by many times over many years, was a memorial to soldiers from Greenpoint who died in WWI. On the marble plinth were the names of towns in Picardie where battles had been fought. I recognized one, Château-Thierry, as the end station of the rail line I took from the Gare de l'Est to go to Brian's house in Gandelu.

I know he thought I cared for him more than I did. Not that I cared for him less, but in a different way that I couldn't explain. I was so afraid before I left for Paris, in the months after my father died. I felt for him that I was about to jump off of the world, into the unknown, and he held my hand until the last minute. He was a good friend to me.

I remember saying goodbye to New York with Anton, sitting on folding chairs on my rooftop in Brooklyn, drinking beers.

I loved sitting there. The city rose up over the river—a galaxy of windows cut from the shadowed buildings. It was so close.

The voice inside me said, Don't go, you need these people.

For you, it was different. I wanted what you had. You had been dead and had come back to life. I wanted to know how you did it, to follow you back out.

You told me about being dead inside, for years, driven by repetition:

I would look up after what seemed months or years and see this alien in the mirror this thing and id look back and realize how numb I had become . . .

whatever soul there may be   may be fine   now   and may not be . . .

I thought maybe I could be alive again too.

I wanted to write a poem so beautiful you would return.

I began in response to a line in a poem you sent me [difficult to excerpt]:

The beginning honest feeling, even if wholly misunderstood, becomes as contrived as possible in later descriptions . . .

I wanted to be honest about how I loved you. This was my wager: if I could find the perfect words, you would not doubt me.

I promised Pascal: *the order of the book is to be the order of thoughts in the mind,* yet I returned here, to this page, again and again. I could not make it right.

I don't understand, or am not ready to say how I loved you. I am writing this to know it. To tell you I loved you and never to do it again.

I may not conceal the order of my thoughts, and am compelled to follow them where they go, but I left openings where I was concealing the thoughts themselves, or when I didn't understand, so I could return to them. This is one such opening. There are two others.

As I wrote, it became clear that I would fail: it would not be perfect; you would not return.

The stakes changed: I could not stop writing until I told the truth.

The last thing one settles upon writing a book is what to put in first, Pascal also says, without contradicting himself. The last thing I have settled upon is you.

This was the beginning honest feeling: I would think of you and smile. It was funny, because I knew you only at a distance, through your writing, our correspondence—but when I thought of you, I would smile.

I taught out in a district of the former East Berlin— Hellersdorf, one of the *Neubaugebiet* [new building districts] suburbs, made up entirely of *Plattenbau*, large concrete housing slabs constructed in the 1970s and 80s.

On the way home, I liked to sit facing backwards in the train car, and lean my head against the window, to watch the rows of *Plattenbau*, stark in the snowy fields of the open countryside they had been so hastily left in, flicker out in the distance—an infinite series, unfolding as in a flip book.

One of the days, I thought of you and smiled.

You were so far away; I had never seen your face. I hadn't spoken to you in months. I thought—Ok, so see what happens.

It was the same for me, you said, when I told you this story. I could hear you smile over the phone, from Texas, when you said it:

I wonder about you, I wonder where you are, what you are doing—I think about you and smile.

I want to be honest about this. I was not alive; I felt nothing. I rode my bike through Humboldthain Park every day, past the frozen *Krokus*-meadow, the small green sign warning not to walk there so that the flowers could grow:

Krokuswiese / Bitte nicht betreten! / Die Natur wird es ihnen danken [Krokus meadow / Please do not enter! / Nature will thank you].

The first flower to return is the *perce-neige*, then the *Krokusse*, the daffodils, *narcisse*, blue hyacinth, the tiniest bluebells in rows on small green stalks.

It's funny that the *perce-neige* is sent first to pierce the snow. The green stem is so thin it can't hold up the white bell of the head, which droops forward. But this fragile thing comes through the frozen ground first. Later, the *Krokuswiese:* a meadow of purple bulbs with orange tongues.

I had first seen brightly dressed African women in *boubous* with babies wound around their backs—a great contrast to the grey of Paris and the sober colors worn by the French—filling buckets with water from a standpipe on the rue de Turenne, in the chic and trendy Marais, and wondered what they were doing there.

Later that summer, there was a fire in a squat around the corner on the rue du Roi-Doré [the street of the golden kings] and seven migrants, *sans-papiers*, from the Côte d'Ivoire died, among them four children. They had been living there in what the French call "insalubrious conditions," without running water and with pirated electricity, the dangerous wiring of which had caused the fire.

E. M. Cioran, who moved to Paris when he was 26, and, after a brief return to Romania in 1941, lived there until his death, wrote:

Switching languages at at the age of thirty-seven is not an easy undertaking. In truth, it is a martyrdom, but a fruitful martyrdom, an adventure that lends meaning to being [for which it has great need!]. I recommend to anyone going through a major depression to take on the conquest of a foreign idiom, to reenergize himself, altogether to renew himself, through the word. Without my drive to conquer French, I might have committed suicide.

To choose to live in another language is a renunciation, a place to hide, a screen between you and the world. For me, the new language was a kind of suicide.

The entire exile, the leap into the unknown, was a gesture of suicide, an offering in lieu of suicide, or in deferral of suicide.

When I look back though, I had many good things around me, which are now destroyed.

Packing my books, deciding which to ship and which to sell, was brutal as I dismantled my life in New York. When I could no longer choose I would say: *Lose farther lose faster*, and continue to jettison ballast.

I speak badly, with a strong American accent, but I am proud of it, of having learned it.

I took classes at a community center that accepted *sans-papiers*, taught by the most kind volunteers [Pierre! Serge!] that cost only 20 euros per year.

In the class were Brazilians, Tibetans, Turks, an Argentinian, Romanians, Bulgarians, a Russian, a Moldovan, and a Canadian.

The women worked as *au pairs* or home health workers, the men worked on the buildings, in restaurants, in the jobs French people won't do. The Canadian, like me, taught English.

Together we spoke a made-up kind of French, with phrases often arranged in the grammar of our native languages, plus our mistakes—which were contagious to each other—and we learned it together. They were patient with me, and kind, as I was the slowest in the class.

Serge would tease me about my American accent, and tell me I looked like Emily Brontë. He would imitate me speaking French—it sounded like a slow, loud cowboy with a French accent. He had a house in a small village outside of Toulouse, the most beautiful village in France, he would tell us, and I would think about going to live there with him.

They knew nothing about me, and had to like me [or not] for myself alone. I remember it was such a relief, after New York.

One of my last days in Bed-Stuy, I was walking on
a rundown street with brownstones and abandoned
homes. On the roof of a derelict wood-framed house,
I saw a wooden coop and a man birding—the pigeons
wheeling above him. The sky over Brooklyn is flat and
blue and open. From streets that run north, one can see
the silver skyline, a mirage in the distance down the hill.
The muezzin calls the prayer on a scratchy loudspeaker
from storefront mosques, and the bells of the many brick
churches ring on Sundays. Ok, New York. Enough.
Goodbye.

I came out of therapy and walked north along the
Hudson, the low winter sun silver through black trees—
one could see the bluffs of New Jersey clearly. The river
must have been warmer than the clear cold air, because
from the surface rose a grey mist, a rolling fog along the
river as far as I could see, to the George Washington
Bridge, a cloud almost as high as the span of the bridge.
Well, I thought, you are alive now anyway.

Peonies are my favorite flowers. Like dahlias, I love their big pendulous heads. Each soft leaf unfolds like a soft cabbage.

I can't have sex with people I don't care about. I don't have to love them, but I have to have some feeling for them or tears will come. The first time I had sex with Eric, some tears came out. You are raining, he said [*il pleut / tu pleures*].

Later [and now still], we were friends. He bought me a bouquet of peonies for my birthday and taught me the word *pivoines*.

I have not had sex with many French men, but they all
had a similar technique, focused on the pleasure of the
woman, from which their satisfaction seemed to derive.
It was a point of honor, in each case, that I should come
first, and again. In French porn too—the woman is laid
on the bed, the ground, the woodpile, her skirt is pushed
up and her panties are pulled off. The man licks her until
she comes. They put their soft lips right up on your clit,
like they know where it is and how it works, and gently
move their tongue across it until you come. Then, they
fuck you. Not like boys who fuck in a pounding sort of
way [which has its own charms], but like men whose job
it is to make you come again.

This sexual bravado is a performance of personality which conceals, but is also part of, a more kindly person within.

To a well-known contemporary critic of his book, *Repetition*, Kierkegaard responded:

The quotes you have selected all come from the first part of the book, where nothing of import happens . . . Everything crucial that is said about repetition is in the second part of the book . . . and to arouse the reader's attention it is again entitled "Repetition."

Whatever is said before is always only a jest or only relatively true, adequately illustrated by the fact that I who said it despair of the possibility . . .

The second part of the book does not explain the fact of the first, but performs a repetition.

Repetition is our task for freedom, writes Kierkegaard, and I am trying to be free—to put something down.

The exile, isolation, the language—was a rupture with
the human world, a clear pane, which hardened and
yet grew more lucid in time. I was less and less able to
make meaningful human contact, but could see more
clearly the life of the others, the living, from which I was
separated.

The new language has no memory stored in it, one
moves only forward into it, and it requires such attention
to the present, such great care to move around, that
memory is, or can be, held off for a time.

It also afforded a barrier of great privacy. As Gertrude Stein wrote, *I have liked all these years to be all alone with my English.* I liked to be alone too, alone with my thoughts, quiet in my head, as the sound of spoken French moved around, but was less able to penetrate, the barrier of my consciousness.

I regret the loss of calm and solitude of having no thoughts in your mind but your own. The world stops at the border of your being—an impermeable membrane as the strange words rise and fall like birdsong—a wash of language around you like weather.

It was such a relief to be alone with my thoughts—though I can't claim to be thinking anything at all most of the time.

On the night train from Paris to Trieste, I could not
sleep, and sat reading in a red leather booth of the
café car through most of the night. As the train exited
the tunnel under the Alps into the bluest hour before
dawn, when the shadow of the world is cast before
itself by the sun coming up over the curvature of the
earth—reflecting itself to itself—the mountains rose up
behind the deep blue air as massed black shadows, and
the moon shone on the glacial lakes around them. Along
the base of the mountains, at the edge of the water, the
lights of what must have been small towns glittered in
the night, and it looked as though stars had slid from the
sky, down the mountains, to drift along the edge of the
mirrored lakes.

I am often awake at this time, and wondered why the atmosphere was so blue in this hour, as the sun rose from behind me in the east, first casting the blue earth shadow before it, then, as it rose higher, the windows and granite of the city would turn from blue to a golden pink as they reflected the sun back to itself, before emerging fully into themselves: the buildings granite, the windows flat and opaque.

The troposphere is thus like a retina, containing the inverse image of the world within itself.

The troposphere is blue, as is the aether which fills it: a soluble medium, once believed to be a substance which filled all of empty space.

Do you comfort or prevent us?

It was the same from my window in Paris—the Eiffel Tower, which I could see across the city in the west, changed colors according to the position of light in the sky. In the early eastern light, it was blue, becoming a flat steel as the morning rose, and when the weather was grey, as it most often is in Paris, the tower was a dark iron, almost black, darker than the clouds and sky around it: a cage of sky, latticed in and through the clouded air.

It was so changeable, I thought it must be made of sky, just a condensed cage of deeper sky in which the larger sky could be caught and admired as it passed.

Just as I had in New York, I sat at the window and wrote down what I saw in the sky, and how the light changed the things I saw. An exact description of the world is a futile endeavor, but I wanted to engrave these images in my mind:

The tower is black if the light of the pearl-grey sky is in the west—a dome of cloud over the city, a rim of pink sky and clear blue clouds lifted below it, over the blue hills of the western suburbs.

The low clouds were a world in reverse: like looking up through grey ice at the surface of a frozen lake, yet *transperced* by birds.

The Eiffel Tower belongs to me, the Beaubourg [the inside-out museum] belongs to me, the silver towers of La Défense, pink in the sunset: these belong to me. This is a list of things I have lost.

I was asleep so long I forgot my life until I heard you.

There was a story on the radio about a girl named Emily and her boyfriend, about how much they loved each other. Emily was hit by a truck, and the doctors in the hospital thought she would die. She could not see or speak or hear: she was alive but there was no way to reach her.

Her mother held her hand and read to her from *The Bridge to Terabithia*, a book she had read to her when she was a child: *There is a bridge*, the mother spoke to her, *between this world and the next, and the bridge is love. I will love you for all eternity.*

If they could not find a way to reach Emily, she was going to be put away in a home. The boyfriend remembered the story of Helen Keller and took Emily's palm and wrote letters on it with his fingers—he spelled out: *I love you.* She answered: *You love me?*

She kept saying: *Pull me out of the wall pull me out of the wall.* Later in the show, she explained that she was in a dark world, and thought she was trapped in a wall.

Just a few weeks earlier, before all of this, as I was losing you, had already lost you, I went to Brighton Beach with Lisa and Luis, and Lisa did the *I Ching* for us. I had never had a reading before, and the question I asked was about you.

The name of the reading was: *The Time of the Skinning is Truly Great.* It said that we would unleash great creative forces in each other.

Répétez, s'il vous plaît—repeat yourself if it pleases you.

I had not meant to repeat myself with you.

Haven't forgotten about any of it, you wrote—one line in February.

It had been a terrible winter in Berlin: it snowed for months. It was dark all day, the sun rose at nine and set at three, and what passed between I would not call day at all, just *grau*. I remember a day on the train: there was a thaw in the ice, the sun was on my face, and the train swept in a circle around the city from the west, through the frozen *Kleingärten*: the little garden plots with sheds and gnomes, and, in summer, enormous flowers: *Sonnenblume, Pflaumenbaum,* giant dahlias, tended so assiduously by the Germans. I was so fucking dead.

I replied in April: It was a difficult winter in Berlin. You were so happy to hear from me.

I am ashamed to still miss you so—you were always so
far away.

I loved you first through your poems. Through the year-
long correspondence—between Texas and Paris—later,
Berlin: poems, emails, later—phone and Skype.

It's all we have, you said, for now.

You sent your poems. I sent my own in return.

I am busy breathing in your thoughts from [the poem] *at the
moment . . . I like to have your words to speak, and feel and have
in my ear,* you wrote *. . . here is Kant and his dove for you while
I continue . . .*

It's so romantic it's like a movie, Brigid said.

She also said, You could not have loved him if he had
not been so far away.

It's not really fair to love the part of a person you see in a poem. Poems are just a performance of the self—a highly selective one at that, as one moves between confession and deflection. But you are the most honest poet I know.

I didn't know you could just tell the truth about yourself.

A poet and not an honest man, says Pascal.

Dearest Rebecca,

I have been banging my head trying to find a way to get to Berlin. I would truly like nothing more. Surprising to say in some ways as we have never met (and so with all the potential pitfalls involved in such a first meeting), but all of this has been nicely surprising . . .

I like the Skype idea. I would like to see your face and hear your voice.

Your face was so open, kind—Oh, you're beautiful, you said.

I closed my eyes and turned my head down and to the left. A small gesture—a deflection of intimacy—I have no control over this flooding [shame].

I pointed to a copy of Kierkegaard's *Repetition* on the bookshelf behind you. You took it down to show me. I put it there so you would see it, you said.

I thought—Oh, he looks like a guy from Texas.
I liked your face, later.

What shall we conclude then, from all our darkness, asks Pascal, but our unworthiness?

People can hide and be hidden in ways outside of physics, you wrote me in a poem.

I can't *know* you, you said once—There is something unknowable about you.

I didn't know what you meant. I had pretended so long I forgot.

I asked you which was the Kant with the dove that flies through space and you answered:

The light dove, cleaving the air in her free flight, and feeling its resistance, might imagine that its flight would be still easier in empty space.

The bird imagines free flight but cannot imagine falling for years up into the sky. No one can imagine this: night and time as one long fall. What do you know of falling? What do you know? The whole weight of the sky holds you up and covers you.

[*Jahrlang ins Ungewisse hinab*]

[*le saut dans le vide*]

[all that is missed from the flying machine is the life of the bird itself]

The poems in *Lichtzwang* were arranged by Celan in the order of their composition. The last of his books to be prepared for publication by Celan himself, it appeared in July, 1970—three months after his suicide.

The title has been translated into English, variously, as:

Lightforce
Lightduress
Lightstrength
Lightcoercion
Lightcompulsion

And into French [by Celan himself] as: *Contrainte de lumière* [*Constraint of Light*].

In all matters of Celan, I defer to Pierre Joris, and prefer his translation of the title as *Lightduress*.

As Celan once said, speaking to his friend Edmond Jabès of a French translation of his poems, It is difficult to do any better.

I think the title contains a reference to Freud's concept of *Wiederholungszwang,* most often translated as, repetition compulsion.

To translate *zwang* as strength, or force, misses the compulsory nature of the repetition, of the light. It is not the power of light at stake here, its strength, but its dominion.

One is forced *by* light, put under duress by light—forced to comply.

I know I don't have the right to speak of him, to compare my life in any way with his. Even to use the word "exile" is shameful in comparison. I would only like to say that I considered him my friend, and thought of him often.

The book was composed as Celan cycled through the various treatments for depression common in the 1960s: electroshock, chemotherapy, repeated hospitalizations and therapeutic supervisions.

Chemotherapy for depression? My students are astonished when I say this. I wonder what will be said of us later, all the pills we took—the increasing amounts of Klonopin I take to drag me down into sleep, an undertow that pulls me down in the day, when I am still tired all day.

I remember this from the last time I lived in New York too: the drugged feeling, the increasing compression and exhaustion—just to get through each day is enough.

The only pity, writes Freud in "The Theme of the Three Caskets," *is that with this explanation we are not at the end of the matter. The question is not exhausted . . .*

If we have the courage to proceed in the same way, he continues, *we shall be setting foot on a path which will lead us first to something unexpected and incomprehensible, but which will perhaps, by a devious route, bring us to a goal.*

I think it's funny when Freud admits that he doesn't know where he is going, and invites the reader to accompany him [if we have the courage!] into the unknown—as though he is saying: Let's go this way and see what happens.

There are three caskets—three children—three things they hold—one holds the silence—she hides so that she cannot be found. Hiding and being unfindable, Freud explains, is another unmistakable symbol of death in dreams.

In some families the question arises as to who is to be sacrificed, who is to be silenced, and who is to be sent away. Death is the transformation, the sacrifice which frees the others.

Some people kill themselves all their lives, the doctor said. But each time the daughter would try to die, the father would rescue her.

. . . *At that moment,* Freud tells us, *the brothers are changed into ravens, and disappear, together with the house and garden* . . .

The girl, he continues, *who is once more ready to save her brothers from death, is now told that as a condition she must be dumb for seven years, and not speak a single word.*

How does the silence of the daughter redeem the others? I would like to know what secret she keeps.

She submits to the test, which brings her herself into mortal danger. She herself, that is, dies for her brothers, as she promised to do before she met them. By remaining dumb she succeeds at last in setting the ravens free.

The silence is the bargain, the wager upon which life depends, for to break this silence would bring ruin [and salvation]. To hide and be hidden, to be silent, is to withhold oneself from the world, and it is by this secret you are bound to the others: you are, in fact, responsible for their lives.

This contract, says the doctor, is as old as you are—it is as old as time.

[The man on the radio said, I brought some tools and forced open the coffin to see my brother again. I brought a bouquet of flowers (and a small book) to put in his hands.]

[*Le monde irréel de l'exil*] The unreal world of exile, in which life is deferred and years pass emptied of content and duration—the peace of total anonymity.

These fragments are pieces of time. I resist the urge to build something with them, but rather hope to approach the same problem, again and again, from many perspectives.

The taxonomic impulse of Linnaeus is common to those who hold the world to be an order reflecting the mind of God. The plants and creatures are arranged in a system of Aristotelian logic: kingdom, genus, and species.

The learning of the new language becomes taxonomic, as orders of genus and species are organized out of nothing, as on the first day, when the names are distributed.

The kingdom emerges, object by object, until you begin to be able to link the objects and move among them, slowly at first, moving from one phrase to another into the unknown, without knowing what you will construct next. I'm never sure where I'm going with this. Just getting to the end of the sentence was enough.

One gathers the pieces slowly, and is concentrated on the gathering, until the day when you have walked into this new world, imperceptibly, and can move freely between the two. My students noticed it before I did, that I could now understand them, and that their conversations were no longer hidden to me.

The learning of the new language is not taxonomic,
but more like the nocturnal wanderings through Paris,
marked on the *Plan de Paris*, in which some districts are
traversed on a regular basis, and all the streets are filled
in and drawn over again, so that the buildings and sights
of the route are clear in your mind and can easily be
recalled, in order, and some districts are visited rarely,
if at all, and one has only a vague picture of the outer
environs.

The landscape is not colored in object by object, but
driven by verb, in motion, through the city which invents
itself, unfolding before you as you arrive—and so you built
a new interior landscape—a whole city without memory.

Grammar is the taxonomy—a system imposed upon language to organize it. Language exists before grammar, and just as children learn their native language without knowing its grammar, you will never learn this new system, this language, this culture, without careful attention to its rules, which will always be alien to you.

Watching for clues to behavior is a skill you mastered as a child, and it is useful here in the strange land too, where you also guess at what is normal in relations between people.

Across from my window was the church and rectory of
Saint-Ambroise: the two steeples framed my view of
the sky and I could look into the large windows of the
rectory. The priest in the window fixes his collar, surveys
the sky, then sits in a chair and begins to read.

The roof of the rectory is light grey, the doves [*colombes*]
on the roof a slightly dun-colored grey, with white collars
like the priest.

I could see in the distance where the rain clouds were:
each metal filament clear as it was swept in veils by the
clouds.

How can you leave all of this? It takes a long time for a
place to live inside you. The film of Paris moves inside
me, at the speed of a bicycle, unfolding in the direction
I choose.

Rain moves across the city in veils—the tower a dark grey of solid cloud. Blue shows through a hole in the southwestern sky. As the rain arrives around it, the tower turns to rain too and disintegrates into mist. The unarticulated lines blend together, dissolved in rain.

I could see the rain coming over the city, the clouds trailing fine metal filaments: this was the rain. I could see then from where the rain was coming, and in which direction it was headed, and so knew where to plan my bike rides. I also grew able to time its arrival: for example, when it was over the tower, moving east, it would take about twenty minutes to reach me.

Leonardo DaVinci wrote in his notebook, *Faces are more beautiful in cloudy weather.* Paris is too. As the sky becomes a grey mass behind the tower, the church before me lightens to grey, and I see for the first time that the cock weathervanes on the tips of the steeples are an oxidized green, shining, irradiated against the grey sky.

As the sky lightens, the tower darkens, and the oxidized green cocks turn grey again, the church resumes its quotidian sandstone, with dark-grey shingled roof.

19:30 Streams of gilded pink [*dorée*] cast by a white light coming from a crack in the cloud directly above the tower—*la lumière de Dieu*. The tower is black, like a rain cloud, the lines less filigreed and distinct.

19:45 Sky a silvered pink behind the tower, the light of God a halo around it, the tower becomes more solid, *mais encore comme une ombre.*

20:00 Sun just above the tower, white silver bright sky behind, the black tower like shadow—filigreed, etched, not solid or transparent—delicate rim of clouds with big gaps of blue between them, the sun behind a luminous cloud directly above the tower.

20:30 Turns blue at sunset—the dusk a pink rim around the perimeter of the city. A grey-blue cloud descends two-thirds down the tower, the lower third pink horizon behind.

8:35 Morning sun in the east: flat grey metal.

Mailing boxes at the post office, a woman on line behind me heard my accent and introduced herself as a fellow American: How long have you been here? she asked.

Four years.
Ah, four will be ok. After seven you cannot leave.
[She had been there twenty.]
I know but I am afraid I will break my heart forever.

L'Abîme des Oiseaux
[to be inserted here]

Produced by the grief of solitude

Injustice:

Devant sa fenêtre du Palais-Royal, Colette contemplait les pigeons et les moineaux s'ébattant au soleil.

—La plus grande injustice qui existe peut-être dans la création, fit-elle, c'est que certains possèdent des ailes.

Aux écoutes, juin 1948

Injustice:

Before her window in the Palais-Royal, Colette contemplated the pigeons and sparrows frolicking in the sun.

—The greatest injustice that exists, perhaps in all of creation, she said, is that some of us possess wings.

Aux écoutes, June 1948

Repetition
[*Le Saut dans le Vide*]

[It was only like that for a time.] Those in exile lead often marginal lives, hiding from something at home, as I was. I didn't know if I wanted to live like that—always the other, inside a strange culture, the raised eyebrow every time you spoke, the silence within and around you. But you get used to it—you get to like it.

Soon after I arrived in France, a young man named Ilan Halimi was tortured and murdered in a *cité* outside of Paris. He worked in a cell phone store on the Boulevard Voltaire, just up from my house.

A gang from the *cité*, known as the *gang des barbares*, hatched a plan to kidnap a Jew and hold him for ransom. They sent a young woman, henceforth referred to in the news as *l'appât* [the bait], into the store to flirt with and lure Halimi. She gave him her phone number and arranged to meet him later.

Halimi was found by the side of the railway tracks *près de la gare de Sainte-Geneviève-des-Bois* naked, hands cuffed behind his back, burned over 80% of his body, and died *en route* to the hospital.

For three weeks, he was held and tortured in a boiler room of the *cité de la Pierre-Plate à Bagneux* [*Hauts-de-Seine*]. The gang repeatedly called Mr. Halimi's family to demand a ransom, and when told the family could not meet their demands said: Go ask the other Jews.

Two French police officers flew to Ivory Coast yesterday on the trail of Youssouf Fofana, the suspected gang leader who had reportedly flown back to his native country after the murder. According to police, Mr Fofana had called himself the "brain of the barbarians."

I remember when Fofana was brought to the Palais de Justice to be held for trial by long rows of blue vans with flashing lights and the hi-lo siren.

The day of the verdict, lines of police, some in full riot gear [high plastic shields, scaled body-armor, and small, pointed, cloth caps set atop their heads—their dark-blue pants slightly bloused above high lace-up boots], blocked the roads around the palace.

I stopped on my bicycle to watch them from the Pont Saint-Michel, after they redirected me from the road along the *quai*.

[It was only like that for a time.] Less and less able to bear closeness of any kind, I grew hideous to myself, as the isolation and depression I had left behind began to catch up with me.

The few friends I had, good friends, I held myself apart from, disappearing for weeks at a time, not returning phone calls, progressively more solitary and numb.

I am ashamed of my loneliness, how it kept me safe for so long.

Repetition is a way to manage time, to parcel time. I divided my time rigorously into manageable increments which grew smaller and smaller over time: the nocturnal wanderings, the swimming at night in the blue-nocturne, chocolate-covered Pim's with raspberry filling while watching French television [anesthetized and lonely, a star-occluding white], wine.

This aether seeps into whatever soul, or vacuum, exists within you. I suspect depression is an evolutionary adaptation. When suffering becomes overwhelming, the anesthetized subject is immobilized, and thus prevented from destroying itself.

Le Lotissement du ciel is a book I love by Blaise Cendrars, translated as: *Sky: Memoirs* [who knows why], or, more literally, as: the parceling, or division, of the sky. What is lost is the sense of division and distribution in *lotissement*, as in the division of a property into lots, or the division of a town into yards.

Le Lotissement du ciel is to apportion the sky—to divide the sky in portions and then distribute those portions.

The sky is time we divide. The sky and time and God are one blue thing that we live in and measure. *For what does time differ from eternity,* asked St. Augustine, *except in that we measure it?* It is birds who apportion the sky, dividing and distributing it among us.

[It was only like that for a time.] One can only run so far, so fast. Eventually, it catches up with you—as my brother says, repeatedly, wherever you go, there you are.

One can only run so far, so fast. What you think chases you lies patiently within you, waiting for you to stop, to pull you down into yourself.

What you ran from you carried within you all of this long way, and herein lies the origin of the story of the birds: how they lay in wait within you, whose wings you could feel flutter in panic whenever you were still, and what it cost you to hold them down.

Later I may tell you how I came to put it down:

How the birds, easily frightened, hum like low continuous
fear-motors now, held in the hand with still wings
[Klonopin], and have moved up higher in my chest,
beneath the collarbone, and no longer live in my lungs
and heart. But many terrible things will happen between
then and now, and this is not a story of redemption.
Suffering is worthless. I am not redeemed; I am not
burned clean.

This a story of repetition, told through recollection. Therein lies the sorrow of it. As Kierkegaard tells it:

Repetition and recollection are the same movement, except in opposite directions, for what is recollected, has been, is repeated backward, whereas genuine repetition is recollected forward. Repetition, therefore, if it is possible, makes a person happy, whereas recollection makes him unhappy.

The meditation at the end of yoga class said, There is no surer path to suffering than the wish to know *why* things happened as they did.

Luis said, If your house burns down, don't kick around in the embers. Keep going.

The doctor said, Don't kick around in the graves of memory, let them lie, let them lie.

The man on the radio said, Be kind, each person you meet carries a terrible burden.

I would like to take memory and cut it from my head.

The first year, I exchanged apartments with a girl who lived on the Île Saint-Louis: a small island in the middle of the Seine, just behind the Île de la Cité, where Notre-Dame is. The half of the island closer to Notre-Dame is more touristic, and the small bridge between the two is often crowded with tourists, watching mimes and musicians, from Easter to September.

Once you cross the rue des Deux-Ponts, which divides the island in two, the street calms and becomes like the main street of any French village—with a butcher, a baker, a cheese shop, a church, a pharmacy with its illuminated green cross, and a post office. My windows were ten feet tall and opened like great doors onto the narrow street and the church and school directly across. The bells of the church woke me in the morning, along with the sounds of the children entering the school.

It was a five-minute bike ride, over the Pont de la Tournelle, from which one can see the Eiffel Tower around a bend in the river, behind Notre-Dame, to the Piscine Pontoise—the pool where Juliette Binoche swims in the film *Blue*. I joined the pool with their *formule nocturne*, which sounds romantic, and means you may join at a reduced tariff if you only swim after 8pm.

The pool was constructed in the 1930s, in the Art Deco style, and looks like a Roman bath, with two tiers of colonnades surrounding the pool, behind which are wooden bathing cabins. The pool glows a luminous blue at night, and the moving lights of the water are reflected against the roof, made entirely of glass, whose windows may be opened in fine weather.

The first time I saw *Blue* was years before I moved to Paris, when I had a boyfriend who liked to watch movies with subtitles. I also visited Paris for the first time with this boyfriend, who did not love me, and I was ashamed to be in such a beautiful place with him.

Though I was unhappy, I knew nothing of grief, but I thought the film was lovely, and remembered mostly the images of Paris and the blue light in it, and how I loved the apartment with atelier windows she moves into alone, with the blue chandelier, on the street I would come later to recognize as the rue Mouffetard.

I sought out the pool specifically for this reason. I remember seeing the film later, on French television, without subtitles, and thought how I could now understand two things I had not before: the new language, grief—two things difficult to translate.

The best I can do for now is to say it was like passing through a transparent film, similar in density and viscocity to a soap bubble, which had covered your world, but disintegrated upon contact.

Once you had passed through to the other side of this film, you could see the other world clearly, but could not explain it to those left behind. It was like it was like it was like this [it wasn't like anything]. I could not return to the time before all of this.

To swim, for me, is also to be without thought—I would count each stroke and lap in French, or conjugate verbs in my head, and so my attention was absorbed completely into the activity. A man I spoke to at the pool, one of my pool friends, said to me, *J'adore la sensation de mon corps dans l'eau* [I love the feel of my body in the water]. I love this feeling too; I love being a mammal who can swim.

In the film, the woman leaves her life after the death of her husband and daughter—she wishes to become anonymous and leave the past behind her.

I understood, in retrospect, why she ran from her old life. If she was alone, she could live without memory, leave memory behind. You think you can escape from memory but you can't.

The doctor said, They are sorry when they learn what they have lost. What is lost in depression and exile is time. Both exist outside of time, but when you return, if you ever return, time has gone on without you. You want to go home, but there is no home. What is lost to me is time. What is lost to me is home. You can never retrieve the lost time.

The thing is, and I dislike this word, but once you expatriate yourself, the home you left ceases to exist, and when you return, if you return, you are separated from it irrevocably by time.

Each new place becomes a search for home, and each new place moves you farther from the original home.

You are a bird with the string let go. Once you accused me of being a person who just goes.

Am I a person who just goes? I will let you know.

Archimedes asked only for a place to stand. His request is alternately translated as, *Given a place to stand [and a fulcrum], I would move the globe.* Or, *Give me a place to stand and with a lever I will move the whole world.*

Philosophers call this fulcrum, or lever, the Archimedian point, and it has come to represent the search for one place of certitude in which to stand, a firm place of grounding from which one may insert a fulcrum beneath the globe and have the force to displace it.

Archimedes, wrote Descartes, *to draw the terrestrial globe from its place, and transport it elsewhere, asked for nothing but that one point be fixed and sure. So too shall I have the right to conceive of high hopes, if I am so happy as to find only one thing which is certain and indubitable.*

The problem with metaphysical systems is this: there is no one place to stand. It is not possible to stand outside of the world, as God does, and shift it with a lever.

One is unable to view life from outside of life, as God might, unable to exist outside of time—just as it is impossible to describe depression from within depression, or to remember that an outside exists.

Nothing exists outside of it.

It may seem that these references are intellectual gestures of deflection, but they are not. There is no difference between what I think and what I feel, there is no sure place to stand, and I am an animal—not a mind who lives in a body—and yet, in *City of God*, St. Augustine tells us, The way in which minds are attached to bodies is beyond man's understanding, and yet, this is what man is.

In his *Meditations*, Descartes too looks for a place to stand [I think, therefore I am], and so becomes the philosophical fall guy, the patsy, the one who divides body from mind.

But, as with many books more spoken of than read, the *Meditations* are nothing like what I expected. Descartes gives away the things of his world one by one:

Take away my senses, my memory, my soul, my face, my hands, my arms; all this machine composed of flesh and bone that I call my body. Take my soul . . .

until he says: you were my thought—you I could hold when all else fell away, when I was left with nothing.

What am I, he asks, *what am I when I have nothing?*

All philosophy, wrote Novalis, is from a feeling of homesickness—an attempt to be at home everywhere in the universe.

All philosophical systems are failures, and I am homesick for a place that does not exist. Metaphysics is a system constructed of memory.

Narcissism too is a relentless machine—a narrative system that folds everything into itself, yet at once a fragile edifice—easily slighted.

Descartes useless and uncertain [says Pascal].

One of the years, I taught at a school in the chic western suburb of Saint-Cloud. I would take the train from Gare Saint-Lazare in the morning, and as it circled around the west of the city in a ring, through Courbevoie, La Défense, Puteaux, Suresnes, Saint-Cloud, the tracks ran along the edge of the high bluffs, so that you could look out over the valley of Paris, and see the river make a big loop through it.

The village of Saint-Cloud climbs a hill up to the former Chateau Saint-Cloud, and though the castle itself was razed during the revolution, the grounds and gardens remain. At lunchtime, I would walk down the hill to the village and buy a sandwich at a *boulangerie* that had the most beautiful strawberry tarts—with enormous glazed strawberries arranged in a crown over the custard.

The women behind the counter never stopped being mildly suspicious each time I spoke—surprised at the apparition of an American in their bakery, surprised that it spoke French. I'd walk back up the hill to the garden, and sit on a bench in a high terrace overlooking the city from the west—exactly as far in the opposite direction as I could see from my apartment—and thus the city appeared reversed and backwards—as I looked through the globe from behind.

In the distance, behind the tower, the hot-air balloon of Parc André Citroën rose and fell on its tether, evenly but slowly, at irregular intervals, as though a giant child were controlling it.

I remember talking to my brother on the phone. He had recently moved to San Francisco, and we were talking about how lonely we were, and how much we had had to give up, to get away. I'm really lonely, I said, but every day I eat my lunch in the gardens of a chateau, and I look out over the city, and I feel lucky to live here. He said that he felt like that about San Francisco too.

I fell further and further inside myself. A German doctor on the radio said, One must face the past and learn to grieve. This is the first time I have turned around to face the past. I thought I knew. I knew nothing.

Grey pigeon, grey Paris, smiled Paul.

My friend Joe's father died. Walking home from the wake with Lee, I said, If my father died I would die too. He died two days later.

Brigid and Louis drove up from New Jersey to tell me.

I tried to slam the door on them, to get away, but Brigid caught me and held me and I sank to my knees. I kept saying, My dad died and you came to tell me—that's so nice of you, my dad died and you came to tell me—that's so nice of you.

Then the little door closed inside me and I was calm. I thought if I could just hurry, I could get to you in time— I could reach you in time if we just hurried but I sat still and was quiet.

The man on the radio said, It brought us to our knees, then we stood up again.

We drove around the bend of the BQE that curves over the Gowanus Canal, past the giant neon signs on their metal scaffolding, the red steeples of Brooklyn rising toward the park on the hill. The bleached New York winter sky is opaque, milky, a depthless mass. The light seemed different, overexposed, like the layer of protection was gone.

Brigid sat in the back seat with me and held my hand.

The sounds that come from a body in grief have no human protection around them. On television in France, Lebanese women held their dead babies up to the camera after the shelling of Beirut. The children had dirty faces and little cuts on their faces—their bodies limp and floppy as the mothers shook them at the camera. You should have to watch this—everyone should have to look at this, what you have done—they seemed to be begging the cameras. They made the sound of animals being hurt by something they can't understand. Why are you doing this to us?

Something I was unable to know before came up in me. I hesitate to speak of it, wishing to avoid both pathos and shame.

Lately, I have been remembering how my father slept all the time. He must have been depressed too, though I could not see it when he was alive. Depression is a cloud of unknowing, a protection against what we do not wish, or are unable to know.

I don't think anyone in my family could know this thing before, though I suspect my sister knew it first: my mother broke the souls of her children.

It would be better if you do not remember, you said to me, but I do remember.

Before I left, she said to me, You are in every part of my life now, when are you going to stop *hanging around?*

I am leaving for Paris at the end of the summer.

[I always answer her questions as though they were requests for factual information.]

I had to go, to keep her with me.

In retrospect, I was trying to make her be my parent now that my father was gone. You want me to be your father but I can't, she would say; you want some kind of satisfaction from me but you are not going to get it.

She was telling the truth. I would not listen.

But once it was all over, once my father died, it was like the end of some terrible insanity, which had been my family. All the air went out of it. The low constant scream inside just stopped, for me, and it all seemed such a terrible waste.

There was also no reason to continue, as the one person who held it together was gone. He just got tired of catching all the pieces as they fell. My brother, who is not a rat, left too. He said, I don't want to be the only person everybody likes.

So, on the one hand, my mother told me to go and I went. On the other, I needed to get away from them. I was angry though, at all I had to give up, to get away.

If you go away inside yourself, you can wait for it to be over. I went away quietly, but what I was waiting out was my life.

Am I more obedient than the others? Am I more guilty?
We are all gone, as ordered. When I was away I would
sometimes think we were in a waiting game, a tensed
waiting to see which child would kill themselves first.
My sister was way out front, but she always chooses
poisoning as her method, which is the least effective.

A study of suicide in America reveals the winners to be:

Men
Single men
Single working-class white men
Gun
Gun in the mouth

I went with my mother to visit my brother in San Francisco after his son was born. As usual, the tension and despair between us all was unbearable. Walking over the Golden Gate Bridge, he said, I hate being with you so much I want to jump over the rail. I understand this hate, but wish it did not extend to me. Once we were friends.

My mother kept saying: Can you believe he said that to us? Can you believe he said that to us? Yes, I can believe it.

In psychoanalytic terms, this expulsion of the bad thing would bring temporary relief by releasing the tension and hate which had built up between us for so long. Someone is the scapegoat upon which all the hatred is projected—the bad thing that must be expelled from the organism. The problem is—the relief would only be temporary.

This is why I do not do it, and each time I look at the George Washington Bridge, each time I want so badly not to be alive anymore I would feel dizzy with it, I think of my mother. I think: you do not get me.

But most importantly, she must not take possession of my body, and, in death, I would finally have been absorbed into her completely and cease to exist. I did not want her to have my dead body and display it in a box.

In *Repetition*, Kierkegaard writes, I have not gone further, my whole life is in it.

I have not gone further; I am standing in the same place. I have gone deeper—further into the past to retrieve something I left there. I'm not sure what it is yet, but I will tell you when I learn it. My whole life is in it.

It snowed eighteen inches the morning and day of the funeral. In the car on the way to the church, I thought, God must be very sorry for us to have sent so much snow—to cover the edges.

After everyone left that night, I waded out through the snowdrifts to the lake behind our house.

Between sky and snow there was nothing—no clear line dividing above from below—only a particulate atmosphere of diode-orange light, as street lamps and people-light cast up against the low clouds and reflected back down.

It was unclear if particles of snow were detaching themselves from the layer on the ground, or if the disintegrating sky was floating down.

The malignant hum of electricity, from a street lamp, was the only sound.

Fuck you, I said to the sky. Do your worst.

The sky considered this. It retracted a little.

Not yet, said the sky.

[Here is the point I start running.]

The doctor asked to read the poem. He wanted to know what the birds are and I told him not to talk about it [the poem] anymore. Later, in another session, he asked more specifically, Are the birds you?

Back in my apartment, I couldn't feel the birds inside me anymore. I thought he had taken them from me.

The lid of the sky unlatched and swung down to smash me flat into a dimension of black hate. I remembered. I knew something I had always known.

I knew what was inside me and who put it there. I remembered how it felt to be a child, to know that my mother hates me, and to know that this hate lives inside me and is the organizing principle of my being—a black hole at the center of my gravitational field which pulls everything into itself—a field of chaos my personality was constructed around not to know this fact.

Once the birds were gone it all rushed up. I kept saying to the doctor, They took everything from me.

[What did they take from you? the doctor asked.]

In the *Phaedo*, Socrates explains the idea of *anamnesis* [recollection] to Simmias, who is given such excellent lines of dialogue as:

"Quite true, Socrates."

"That is true."

"Very true."

But if the knowledge, replies Socrates, *which we acquired before birth was lost by us at birth, and afterwards by the use of the senses we recovered that which we previously knew, will not that which we call learning be a process of recovering our knowledge, and may not this be rightly termed recollection by us?*

I am not speaking of repetition at all, only recollection.

The summer I arrived in France, two boys died in the suburb of Clichy-sous-Bois. As they were running from the police, they hid in an electrical substation, and were electrocuted. Riots and car burnings lit up the *banlieue*, the poor suburbs which ring the north of the city, and are another world apart from Paris, divided from it by the *périphérique*—the highway which encircles Paris completely—and are like a great ugliness that surrounds, and thus contains, the city to the north, as though the pressure of this ugliness delimits Paris at its border, allowing the beauty of the center to exist, outside of time, in a domed snow globe.

The run-down, graffiti-ridden tower-blocks, some with broken and boarded-up windows, stretch for miles and miles.

None of these places, I should say, look as bad as housing projects in New York.

On the American news each night: Paris is burning!

Friends would call from New York to ask if Paris was
burning—could I see the flames from my window. No,
I looked out the window: I see tourists with ice cream
cones from Berthillon.

The sexy riot police sat in long rows of blue vans eating
takeout from containers along the Boulevard Henri IV,
leading up to the Bastille, across from the arsenal, where
the cavalry of the Republican Guard are stationed, who
ride through the streets on the most beautiful horses,
their manes braided, in uniforms from another century:
high black boots, white riding breeches, short blue
jackets with gold buttons and braided epaulettes, and
gold helmets with flowing red manes. They would pass
under my windows on the Île Saint-Louis several times a
week on patrol.

The demonstrations came to the center, as students protested in the streets near the Sorbonne. I rode my bicycle to watch, and was surprised to see students throwing paving stones at the riot police, who advanced in a line behind plastic shields, and hit the students with clubs.

Every generation, in turn, must *go in the streets*. Revolution is thus tradition in France, and the paving stone is a tradition, just as hitting students with batons is a tradition.

The *Danielles* [Danièle and Daniel] said, What you do not understand is that we are Communists *au fond du cœur* [at the bottom of our hearts]. Dany grew up in the "red suburb"—one of the Communist towns along the northern and eastern borders of Paris—of Ivry-sur-Seine, and every May Day, the International Day of the Worker, which is also my birthday, the children of her school would sing the *Internationale* and release red balloons into the sky, in solidarity with the martyred people of the USSR.

The French news speaks of peaceful demonstrations
marred by a few troublemakers. Sarkozy is Interior
Minister and promises to *"nettoyer la cité au Kärcher,"* and to
get rid of the *"racaille"*—to blast it clean of dirtbags with
a fire hose is the closest translation I can make—but they
have one verb for this [*karcherizer*]. It is a low slang and
a rough way to talk—this is why they pretend not to like
Sarkozy, whom they call *"l'Américain."*

At this point, I have to confess that I have begun to conceal from you the order of my thoughts. I had to circle back around to the repetition, to fill in the blank spaces I had left open. There were many gaps in my memory. I began to be confused the closer I approached it, and so began to wander in my thoughts.

Flaubert once wrote to his most dear friend Louis Bouilhet: Ineptitude consists in wanting to conclude. . . . What mind of any strength—beginning with Homer—has ever come to a conclusion?

So, I promise to continue, but confess it that I grow tired.

The German on the radio said, I do not think metaphors
are helpful. The metaphor in question was Angela
Merkel as *Schwabian Hausfrau*, trying to get her children
to eat their vegetables. What he meant, I think, is that
metaphors are impractical and thus useless, which is such
a very German thing to say, and so seemed funny to me.

The Spanish man on the panel said, Out of the frying
pan into the fire.

The Italian said, If you have good news to present, you
have no need of metaphor.

This is the problem with metaphor: it is an image to hide behind—a place to hide the inexpressible thing you feel. The beauty of the first part was a lie I was telling you about myself.

My father wanted me to be perfect; my mother wants me to be dead. Neither of them is or was conscious of this wish. To be perfect is to be dead. Lyricism is a straining after perfection, a straining into a dark place to pull out small fragments of ash from the ocean, small pieces of light from the sky. See, even now I am unable to prevent myself from it.

The beauty of the first part is a lie, a concealment of all the information that reappears in the second part. Everything of value is to be found in the second part of the book, which I have helpfully named "Repetition," in order to alert you to this fact.

The birds are not me, they are not anything. They're not even birds.

In the Westhafen station in Berlin, a quote from Heinrich Heine is inscribed in the wall and runs in a line of descending tile down the stairs into the tunnel. On the wall to the right, it is written in French, on the left, German, so I would read them as I walked down the stairs to transfer to the U-bahn, and translate one from the other:

Here in France, as soon as I arrived in Paris, my German name "Heinrich" was translated into "Henri," and I had to adapt myself to it and had even so to call myself thus around here, for the word Heinrich was not pleasing to the French ear and the French do make everything in the world very pleasant for themselves. Even the name "Henri Heine" they were unable to pronounce, and most of them called me Monsieur Enri Enn. Many contracted this to Enrienne and some called me Monsieur Un Rien [Mister Nothing].

The disintegration of identity that takes place in migration is caught perfectly by Heine, as is the French national character, which adapts the world to please itself, and not the other way around, and this world is very pleasing indeed. For why should the world not please us?

Again, I would not like to dramatize my situation through the use of the word "exile." I chose to leave. There was not one day that I did not feel lucky beyond measure to live in Paris. There was not one day it felt like my real life.

I had a small, foolish thought that if one lived in a sunny apartment with windows like great doors—what could one possibly be unhappy about?

At the same time, I felt sent away.

The greater sorrow lies in knowing that all of the nicest days of my life happened during this time. I have spoken only of loneliness and grief, but each of these best days was spent with people I love:

1st birthday: Train to Normandy coast to visit the glamorous seaside resort of Deauville with the Brazilians. Learned the word *cerf au volant* [kite], had a picnic on the beach which looked like New Jersey, and ate ice cream from silver goblets in a café on a square with a fountain.

2nd birthday: Visited Justin in Berlin, in the apartment with a view of the steeple. We sat in the grass along the canal and drank wine from plastic cups with the sun on our faces.

3rd birthday: Gandelu with Brian. Took Zoe for a walk and discovered the bower of bluebells: the forest floor a carpet of flowers [*tapis de fleurs de sous-bois*]—each blue head and green stem glowing, singly—dusty light falling through the dim forest. It was the most beautiful thing I have ever seen. Each year we searched for them again, but there was only the small window when they bloomed, and it was only perfect the first time.

4th birthday: Visit Dany's parents in the Ardèche, in the house on top of a mountain, the pine forest behind the house and the giant purple irises growing wild along the road. *Le virage*: motion and altitude sickness caused by veering around precipitous mountain roads in a car. Again, they have one word for this.

5th birthday: Gandelu with Brian and Joël, pink champagne and chocolate ganache cake in front of the fire—long bike rides through the Picardie hills and villages.

And several non-birthdays I would like to add:

Fish and a glass of white wine with Wayne in the *KaDeWe* food court [lunching in a chic department store is like being re-parented], then we walk through the forest of lanterns with Justin.

Snowy Central Park with Bernadette: Christo's orange gates blowing through the paths. The first time I had gone out since my father died, and the gates were like prayer flags on a mountain, flapping in the silent snow.

Madame Moch's with Andy, who gallantly bought her a bouquet of tulips *en route*—all the walks with Andy, through Paris, through Berlin, through New York.

It is not against canon law to be cremated, but you have to bury the ashes. After the funeral my brother said not to tell the priest what we were doing with the ashes—Don't say we're not going to the cemetery.

So that on the last day, the Day of Judgment, we may rise in our bodies to heaven—if we are burnt and scattered, how will God find us?

In the dream God is angry with us for throwing your ashes in the ocean. He tells me you can come back if I pick up every last ash off the ocean floor and put it back in the jar: If you miss even one, you lose.

Ok, but only if I can have him back for twenty years—you can't just give him back to me then take him again.

So I have to go into the ocean to find all the ashes and put them in the jar again.

Ashes fall through the water like sinter, like pieces of light, like metallic powder glinting in the clouded water. I keep trying to catch them, but they keep dispersing.

Ashes drift and spin in the quiet under the curve of the waves. Finally, I can't breathe and wake up [every time].

I dive into the clouded water again, and try to catch the ashes as they sift along the sand, turn in the motion of the waves, and dissolve into the sea.

Don't dream that anymore, my mother says [afraid].

They are sorry when they learn what they have lost. What you came back to retrieve does not exist, but you can gather the broken pieces and put them back inside you. Each fragment is a piece of something I broke and lost.

My father loved birds, and kept a pair of binoculars on the ledge of the bay window in our kitchen that looked out on the lake behind our house. He would watch the birds through the binoculars and report to you when he had seen a particularly interesting one: a pair of snowy egrets, a black swan, a robin redbreast or a blue jay; but mostly the quarreling sparrows ate the seeds he left on a birdfeeder he had hung from a tree before the window.

After he died, Louis said, I'll always remember your father as a gentle giant who loved to watch birds from the window.

This time in New York, the temporary one, is not about retrieving my old life here, it can't be—that life is gone. Instead I walk north, further into the city of my past, to find something I lost there. The walks in the Bronx are a way of visiting my father, of being close to him, and they are about something else too, as though I need to go all the way back in time, to touch something at the very bottom of myself, in order to push up off this bottom and swim to the surface again.

Am I going back to these places to retrieve something I lost long ago—or walking through them one last time?

There was a story on the radio, about a man who spent his life trying to construct a time machine so he could see his dead father again. His father died when he was ten. He was a television repairman in the Bronx, and had a sudden heart attack. You have to understand, said the man on the radio, how much the boy *loved* his father. His day didn't really begin until his dad came home from work. The boy, now a man, said, If he had asked me, *Will you come with me into death?* I would have gone without a second thought.

I know the love this boy had for his father. But I returned here to try to be honest, to myself, about this love—what its requirements were.

I remember how angry he was: a volatile rage, anesthetized by depression, which could, and did, explode at any time.

I think about how he collaborated with my mother to create an airless system of control, and how he never once told her to shut the fuck up. He never told her to stop.

You look like a prostitute, go upstairs and change, he would say to me—later, to my sister.

You girls always had to *please* him, my mother said, after he died.

I hadn't spoken much to my mother in the years before he died. I came home only for holidays, and if I called the house, she would say, Hold on, I'll get your father, and drop the receiver on the counter.

After he died, she said to me once, Every time you walked into a room, he smiled. Her voice sounded flat, tired. Everything you are, you are because of him.

Also around this time, she said, He would always *tell* me how lovely you are.

I must have done something nice for her just then, but I can't remember what.

We were having dinner at Vic's Pizza. There must have been an intimate silence, because she said, apropos of nothing—Maybe that's why he loved you so much—because you are like me.

I started to cry. What, I thought that was a nice thing to say, she said.

Before the wake, Mr. McDevitt told me, When I spoke to your father, he would put his hand on my shoulder, and look into my face, and really listen. It was like you were the only person in the world.

We got tents and heaters to put outside the funeral home for the wake, he said—to hold all the people. I must have looked surprised because he said, Well, it's for your father.

In the afternoon, the line came through for three hours. Because I came home so rarely, a lot of people didn't know who I was. I didn't know he had another daughter, they would say.

We went home between the viewings, to eat. When we came back in the car, we saw the line of people in dark coats, their good coats, around the block and down as far as the church.

When it was over, my sister said, You didn't cry.

Only you and Mommy didn't cry.

My brother was next to me on the receiving line. Mr. McGovern hugged him, and held him tightly, and he started to cry—It's very hard, he said.

I thought, How can you do that? I'd be afraid to: I'd never stop.

We offered no comfort to one another.

One of the last people on line was a mentally handicapped man my father would sit and talk with on a bench after he went jogging in the mornings on the boardwalk. I can't remember his name. The man shuffled along the line, like he didn't understand the protocol: shake hands with the family, say you are sorry. My mother reached out and took his hands. She introduced him to us. I know, I said, my dad would always tell us about you, he always spoke of you. The man said, He was my friend, and started to cry.

The week after the funeral, Doc brought his son over. I can't remember his name. He was nine or ten, I think, and had written a poem about my father. He shook and cried as he read it to me. I remember the poem was about how my dad was a gentle giant who loved everyone.

After my father died, my brother and I had one of several real conversations. We had never spoken honestly to each other before. I think he liked that, my brother said, speaking of my father, how much power he had over people in the outside world, because he could never make us happy.

He also asked me if I thought our mother was crazy. I wanted to make him happy so I lied. Or, I lied because it was easier. Or, I just lied.

When I played basketball in high school my father would sit on the sidelines and shout directions at me as I was dribbling up the court. I wanted to throw the ball at his face. I said he couldn't come anymore then worried about how sad I had made him.

When I stopped eating I couldn't play basketball anyway. I remember thinking, if I could only get to 100 pounds [I am 5'10], then I would be safe. I wouldn't have to worry anymore. I'd have a ten-pound margin of error. I could only get as far as 110.

He was angry at me a lot during these years. There was *a lot* of shouting, my mother said to me after he died, you shouted at me too.

That's not equal, I said to her. That's not equal.

I know, she said.

I could see on her face, just that once, that she did know.

No, there was one other time, after he died:

Your father was very good at that, at making you feel like everything would be ok. I didn't have a lot of that—in my house, growing up—there was a lot of yelling and fighting—your father came and made me feel like everything would be ok.

It was like that in our house too, I said.

I know, she said. I thought I saw fear move behind her eyes.

My mother would creep up to the bathroom door and listen as I vomited rage and my dinner. I don't work so hard just so you can vomit up my food, she would bang on the door and shout. Mostly she would just listen. She would say later, I always know when you are finished, because you cough after.

They had me committed. A nurse on the floor called them and told them to come get me. She had a son in my school, and shamed them into coming back, saying that I just had anorexia, and it wasn't safe to leave me in the psych ward. She sat on the side of my bed and stroked my hair and told me what a pretty girl I was, that I didn't belong there. She stayed with me until they came with a bag of clothes and toiletries and a sandwich, which I ate. I remember not knowing which one of them I had to break to get them to take me home. I was afraid of the other patients.

My parents were angry and embarrassed.

After they relented, and agreed to take me home, I gave part of the sandwich to another patient, a black girl around my age, who was hanging around. She asked for my phone number and I gave it to her.

When she called the house the next day, my mother mocked me for not taking the call. Oh, now you are too good for her aren't you? Yesterday you were giving her your sandwich, and your phone number, so nice, so kind, but today, you are too good for her.

After he died, she said to me, Why don't you ever remember anything *nice*? But there *wasn't* anything nice, I answered.

We weren't allowed to lock our doors. I used to put my bed in front of the door to keep my mother out, so she could not wake me, and so they couldn't conduct random prison searches.

Once, my father tried to open my door and the bed was blocking it. It was after school and I was in my uniform, which I was too tired to bother changing out of [I remember I used to sleep in it], smoking and listening to the radio. He broke the door down and threw the bed over. I remember him hitting the door with his shoulder, slowly, like an elephant, until it cracked open and broke. It stayed like that until the house was sold after he died, almost twenty years later. My sister was six or seven, and her room was across the hall. After he left, she came in and asked, Are you ok?

We would sit together after times like that, and say, I love you more than anyone else in the world.

Later, my mother would say it was my fault that my sister was sick, that I had given her the idea. I was so surprised, she said, when she turned out like you.

One Father's Day, my sister was sitting on the back porch eating the ice cream cake that had been bought for the occasion out of the middle of the cake with a fork. I yelled at her to stop. What the fuck do you think you are doing? That's the cake for dinner! Do you have to eat it out of the middle with a fucking fork? She told me to go away and I would not.

She stood up and came toward me with the fork held like a knife—fist around the handle, tongs down, arm raised in the air. I ran and shut the door to the porch so hard that the handle broke off and she couldn't open it. I stood on the other side, inside, shouting at her [you fucking cunt, you fucked-up bitch, etc.] She made a fist and punched it through the thick glass of the old door, then pulled her arm back out, reflexively, so that it was slit all the way down by the sharp edges of the glass.

I took her to the kitchen sink and wrapped her arm tightly in a dishtowel to try to stop it bleeding so much. I held it up over her head, as she vomited the cake into the sink.

I called Mr. and Mrs. Barry and told them she had had an accident and could they come right away. She was crying and saying that it was my fault—Now I will have to go back to the hospital and it is all your fault. They had a pay phone on the hall at the hospital [I remember my parents were proud it was in Princeton, and used to pretend, vaguely, that she went to school there—I think she was eighteen then], and if you let it ring long enough, one of the patients would answer it and get her for you. I would call every night, and whichever girl answered would go away for a long time, then come back and say, Sorry, she's not here. My parents would go to visit and not tell me. Finally they said, Don't call anymore.

A few years after he died, we were walking through Riverside Park together, after we had gone to see her doctor. I was home from Paris for a visit, and we were talking about my mother.

Well, she loves us though, I said.

She doesn't, my sister said.

Two last memories of New York to leave you with: yesterday on the 1 train, three teenage girls got into an altercation [I don't know how it started] with a woman, who was maybe in her mid-thirties. They were calling her a fat cunt, and one of them was shouting at her, how you even shave the hair on your fat ass you fat cunt. When's the last time you even seen your ass you fat cunt. The young woman, if I may call her that, stood up and moved right in front of the older woman. She put one leg up on the plastic seat next to the woman and mimicked shaving her ass, reaching between her legs and thrusting her cunt in the woman's face. This how you shave your cunt you fat cunt? How old are you even you fat cunt? When's the last time you got some dick you fat cunt? The other two girls cackled around her like hyenas. The woman looked ashamed, and everyone else in the car looked at the floor. Once in the early 90s I saw a crackhead spit in a man's face because he wouldn't give her a dollar. This was worse.

I used to love New York, and I suppose I could not hate it so much now if I had not. One could walk for hours along the Williamsburg waterfront, through the ruined industrial architecture, along Kent and Franklin, and see hardly anyone except the Polish men fishing along the water behind the empty factories and warehouses of Greenpoint, using old spackle buckets for their catch. I remember a type of milky-white fish, swimming along the bulwarks, with bulbous eyes: a pale, sick thing which looked like it had come from some blind cave deep in the ocean.

The light off of the water is still beautiful there though, a bit bluer, a little mistier than elsewhere in the city, in the evening, the blue rising off the moving water, the pink refracted in the windows across the river.

The spines of the books I admired through the windows of the rue Linné were shades of off-white, or light, washed tan, as are most French books, with simple lettering on the covers, in black or red. I loved the eggshell texture of the paper, the woven density of the matte covers, and began to buy books even before I could read them. On weekends, Parc Georges-Brassens in the 15ème has a used book fair, and under the cast-iron pavilions, open at the sides, like an open-air aviary, vendors set up booths with piles of old books.

The first book I bought was by Max Jacob, a book of prose poems from his later spiritual writings, after he converted to Catholicism and became a monk, before he was deported to the internment camp at Drancy, and died there of pneumonia, before he would have been shipped to a *destination inconnue* [Auschwitz].

Across from the fair was a bakery with, in my opinion, the best apple tarts in Paris. The flaky crust left a clear butter stain on the wax paper wrapping, and the apples were lightly caramelized.

As I became able to read, a small thing I had thought was dead moved a little inside me—something that belongs to me. I would visit the bookstore near my house, and buy books recommended to me by the staff there, books about walking in Paris, in *Nord* [*Quartier*], cycling the *Petite Ceinture*—the abandoned rail line that circles Paris. I reread the French poets I love: René Char, Cendrars, Apollinaire, Reverdy—and would try to keep the words only in French—not to translate them into English as I read—an act of concentration that allowed me to exist only in the poem, for that time—to enter a new world in which I met old friends where they lived. I came to them and there was no longer anything between us. Reading took on a new intimacy—slow and precise—as in meditation, as you lightly push thoughts away, only here pushing the English words away.

The meditation at the end of yoga class said, Grief is given to us to know what God knows and to feel what God feels.

I had to put my hand on my forehead to keep it from breaking again. Oh, I first thought, because God holds all the sorrow in the world inside himself.

Oh, but he holds all the love too.

The doctor said, I think your brother holds the rage of your family, your sister is the holder of the insanity, and you are the holder of the despair.

Three parcels divided and distributed among us, each holding a bag of intolerable emotion. That makes it sound, I said to him, like my job is more noble than the others. Perhaps they sit in similar rooms with a doctor who tells them they are innocent—the calm, book-lined antechambers of the Lord in which we are absolved.

Despair, however, is the only mortal sin among them, as one has willfully turned their face from God and lives in darkness.

The first birthday after my father died, Brigid and Louis came over with their four children, and Aidan and Moya with Ciara and Liam. It was a beautiful day, and we sat in front of the house as the children played in the yard, running through the grass in this magical damp green spring light. They found a bird egg and a nest and stood in a circle around it, poking it with a stick. It was so perfect my brother started to cry. Aidan put his hand on his back.

My mother was frantic—asking who said something to him. Did you say something to set him off? [No, it's just that he would have liked this so much.] What did you say to him? Who said something to him?

Why are all of you so angry? she often asks.

When we first saw my father in the open coffin, we were whimpering and patting him like small animals. My mother snuck up beside me and poked me in the side: Look I think he moved, she said. I moved a little away from her. She did it again, poking me, No look, I think he moved.

Later, at the funeral, after everyone had spoken, she leaned over in the pew and said, Why doesn't anyone love *me*?

It's like my mother always said [quoting her own mother, my grandmother], you come into the world alone and you die alone.

When I was a child I would say, But *you* were there when I was born.

She also says, I thought if I got married and had a baby I wouldn't be lonely anymore—but it wasn't true—you'll always be lonely.

A story she tells again and again: When you were a child you had the most beautiful blond hair, and I would brush it every night before you went to bed.

Once, I was brushing your hair, and I said to you: This is the nicest thing I did all day. And you said: You must not have had a very nice day.

Once when I got to the hospital, my parents were having a chat with the nurse, who I'll call Amy, because that was her name.

My sister lay on the bed, tied by her wrists to its high metal sides, writhing and sedated, periodically emerging into semiconsciousness to pull at her restraints and curse at us. The blue hospital robe was falling off her shoulders, and her face and the front of the gown were smeared with the charcoal she had vomited when they pumped her stomach.

Hi! they said when I came in, This is Amy—Amy is married to so and so [some asshole] you went to high school with? Do you remember him? Do you remember him—he was in your year! Yes, Amy said, I'm married to so and so do you remember him? Why yes, yes I do remember him! Everyone was shouting and cheerful.

Amy said, I was going to rub some lotion on your sister, but would *you* like to do it? Maybe it would be nice to rub some lotion on your sister—to make her feel better?

No Amy, no I would not like to rub lotion on my sister. My parents and Amy looked at each other meaningfully over the bed [We're so sorry / I understand].

How things looked on the outside was very important. We lived in a beautiful house on a lake, but it was silent and empty—no food in the refrigerator, broken things were never fixed—nothing worked.

A petty but typical incident: I was looking for scissors to cut wrapping paper with. Stuffed in a drawer there were at least seven pieces of scissors—broken in half, blades or handles broken, too dull to cut. My mother came in and asked what I was doing. Why do you have all these broken scissors, I asked? This is the house of nothing.

She still brings that up: Remember when you called it the house of nothing? Remember when you called it the house of nothing?

Where are we going? I don't know yet. Celan says we are going towards something:

This is how poems travel: orientated towards something; towards something that stands open, that can be occupied, perhaps towards a Thou that can be spoken to, a reality that can be addressed.

I am, oddly enough, not a religious person but a lonely one. Dear addressable unknown, if I speak to you like this, it's only because I have no one else to ask.

The addressable unknown, a *Thou* who inhabits, or who I would like to imagine inhabits, the dark places I address myself to—a small person, shaking her fist at the sky.

You though, *du*, are the first real person I have spoken to in, through, a poem—not to reach beyond something, but to reach you. You are real to me.

I could not turn around before and look at all this mess, all this waste. On the radio, the German doctor says, We must learn to tolerate difficult emotions—remembering can move you forward—if you can extract meaning from horrible experiences.

I keep meaning to return to Stein's happy repetitions, but will have to be content, for now, to repeat a story she tells in *The Autobiography of Alice B. Toklas*, and to say, briefly, that the secret to her good repetitions is that they are no repetitions at all:

We had a few adventures, we were caught in the snow and I was sure that we were on the wrong road and wanted to turn back. Wrong or right, said Gertrude Stein, we are going on. She could not back the car very successfully and indeed I may say even to this day when she can drive any kind of a car anywhere she still does not back a car very well. She goes forward admirably, she does not go backwards successfully.

I am coming closer to the present though, and when I arrive in it, I will stop. I know there is no now; that it will slip from my grasp immediately; that it does not exist— but I will stop anyway.

In this way time is a motion of the soul, and neither exists.

It was not the sky that came unhinged but my mind, which broke, and my body, which folded, hinged at the waist. I could not stand or hold my head up.

I kept saying I know I know I know—I know it now, tell her I know—I think to my sister, by way of apology, for not knowing before.

If you are keeping a secret from yourself, I hope you never learn it.

My project was to try each cheese in the cheese shop, in turn, and each pastry in the bakery: *tarte aux fraise, abricot pistache, framboise, poivre, normande, clafoutis, croissant aux amandes, tarte tatin* . . .

Coming from New York, I could, of course, not cook, so much of the first year was spent putting things on baguettes and eating them. I remember calling Carl, who had lived in France, the first week, and saying, What the fuck am I supposed to eat here—it's like 9 PM and everything is closed.

Carl said, You will have to go to the supermarket and buy and prepare food like normal people. He also told me about the falafel on the rue des Rosiers in case of emergency. There really is no culture of "takeout" in Paris, so when I returned to New York, I was surprised at the delivery men on bikes, flying about like bats, against traffic, who run up and down the stairs of my building in the evenings bringing plastic bags of food to the New Yorkers, who are unable to feed themselves.

French people like to tell you how to do things, and once the people on the island figured out I wasn't going away, they began to teach me how to do the things one must do, and I felt that they were pleased with me, their American child, and my progress.

The *fromager* taught me all the different cheeses, one, he said, for each day of the year. The post-office clerk taught me how to send a package at the lowest rate, the pharmacist and his daughter helped me learn the insurance system, and the bakery ladies worked particularly on my pronunciation, and thought it was

191

funny that I would shout *hello* when I passed them on my bike, as they were out walking their small dogs on the two-hour lunch break all of these establishments took, closed from one to three each afternoon, closed on Mondays.

I had a crush on the butcher and would become shy
when he flirted with me. He taught me the different cuts
of meat and how to prepare them. I only had a hot plate
and a mini oven in my studio, a common kitchen set up
in Paris, but Joël taught me to make soups, fish in paper,
merguez, couscous, leeks, lentils, salads with goat cheese
and beets—things French people make.

In many ways they taught me to be a human again, and
re-parented me in a gracious, slightly amused way.

They were nice to me.

Joël once said to me, *C'était ton papa, et tu es venue à Paris pour faire ton deuil.* [He was your father, and you have come to Paris to make (or *do*) your grief.]

The French phrase *faire le deuil,* to make your grief, is accurate, I think, in its description of grief as a work you must do, rather than a time you submit to, waiting for it to end or pass.

You must make your grief.

I am making my grief.

Walking home, the night before Easter, the day of forgiveness, the streets around Penn Station are mostly dark and empty. A man stands on the corner next to me, leaning up against some scaffolding, wrapped in a sleeping bag, his wild hair and beard matted; his skin is grey with filth, and a milky film of insanity coats his eyes. The second refrain I repeat to myself, silently, sometimes unconsciously, is, *Here is the Lord Jesus Christ who walks among us. Here is the Lord Jesus Christ who walks among us.* He holds all the sorrow in the world inside his body.

The first refrain I repeated to myself, in time with my steps, when I first returned to New York, was, *The victory of Capitalism is largely complete; the victory of Capitalism is largely complete,* sometimes interrupted by—*that's fucking retarded.* I live near Loehmann's, where a sign in the window says, SHOP 24/7, and on the corner is a Pottery Barn—so my block smells like candles and the urine of small nervous dogs. A salon I walk by every day has a picture of a celebrity in the window, her face covered with gold leaf flakes—a new luxury beauty treatment! But it just looks like a golden money shot.

When I get home and turn on the radio, a man on the BBC is interviewing a woman who suffers from spina bifida, which means her spine is severed.

The doctor asks her to rank her suffering on a scale from one to ten. Maybe he asks her this because suffering is indescribable, unquantifiable, because the only way to know what she suffers is to have that suffering imposed on us, forcibly. Maybe it is a stupid question.

She describes wanting to die, attempting to die:

I went to a bookstore and stole *Gray's Anatomy* so I would know how to cut my wrists, so I would know how to do it correctly . . .

I slashed both wrists.
I took a very large overdose of pain relief.
I drank a whole bottle of martini.
I got my favorite teddy bear.
I lay down in bed and waited to die.

At the hospital, she says, the doctors asked for permission to pump my stomach . . . they waited 'til I lost consciousness, then they did it anyway.

The interviewer asks her if she thinks suffering *is* redemptive, if it has value.

Yes, she answers, if I offer my suffering up to God as a prayer . . . it is almost like I am carrying the cross with him, like helping him . . . and by that suffering he manages to redeem us all.

I was in the middle of the way and I lost my way. I've been trying to get home ever since, reckless and falling, running through abject bottomless fear. I am afraid all the time. What would it be to you if I could describe this fear without shame or pathos? I know you know it.

Would it make you love me again?

Would it bring you back?

If I am honest, I wanted you to be my home—the one sure place to stand. Is this something one person can do for another? I don't know. I don't know anything.

The doctor says there is too much blame in my family. It is very important to know whose fault things are. *Es ist meine Schuld,* Germans often say: it is my fault. When I asked my young students, twenty, twenty-one years old, about *Schuld* [guilt], about what is known in Germany as the *Nazizeit,* Felix said, I know that I am responsible but I am not guilty.

The French speak of "bearing the burden of history." Many schools, in the northeast of Paris particularly, bear a small brass plaque which says:

A la mémoire des petits enfants / de cette école maternelle / déportés de 1942 à 1944 parce qu'ils étaient nés juifs, / victimes innocentes de la barbarie nazie / avec la complicité active / du gouvernement de Vichy. / Ils furent exterminés dans les camps de la mort.

In memory of the small children / of this nursery school / deported from 1942 to 1944 because they were born Jewish, / innocent victims of the Nazi barbarism / with the active complicity /of the Vichy government. / They were exterminated in the death camps.

What is my fault? For a long time I thought everything, then: nothing. For a long time I thought nothing. Now I think about it all—how I hurt people, not just myself as I had claimed for so long—by turning away in anger, in fear, in despair.

You could be more honest, I say to myself. Be more honest in your reckoning. *Go farther, go faster.* This is the quality I most admired in you—your honesty. I loved your kind honest voice.

If I am honest, I was a liar and a drunk when we met. I couldn't be close to you or anyone.

I would go to the pretty wine store on my block, the nice German owner, listening to music, candlelight, tastings laid out on a barrel.

What is the music? I asked him, it is so beautiful. *Was hören Sie?* I asked, touching my ear—*es ist sehr schön. Unfassbar schön und traurig.*

Chopin, he answered—genuinely moved. We listened together a few moments.

I would get the cheapest bottle: five euro red Spanish wine—it was a nice wine. He would wrap it in this beautiful, plain paper—pretend it wasn't just for me. Sometimes I'd buy the second cheapest, to pretend as well. Sometimes I'd say, You don't have to wrap it; it's just for me.

My Uncle Tommy, my father's brother, who died a long time ago, used to say, when I was a child, that I had a special soul. My mother told me that story—because she wanted me to remember it.

I used, I think, to be a more kind person, and hope that some part of that kindness remains within me. If I have a soul or I do not, I wish it were not such a hard soul. I just got really lost and broken.

If all that brings me to my knees is grief, then I can say
I am lucky—I live on the right side of history—not the
righteous one, but the lucky one. I am not forced.

It is all that has brought me here, to my knees, where
I am shown a mercy I do not deserve, where I remain,
braced for impact, in repentance for the past, to let
it blow through me, in one last image, as the wind of
outer space vents itself through my core. From here it
is only one more fold, one hinge lower, into the pose of
submission to the past.

Post Scriptum
l'après-coup / Nachträglichkeit / afterdragishness

Lacan is a writer I had avoided until now, as I avoided the dudes who were fond of quoting him in graduate school. So I was surprised, when I began my investigations into repetition, to find that he is quite poetic:

. . . nothing has been more enigmatic, he writes, *than this Wiederholen [repetition], which is very close, so the most prudent etymologists tell us, to the verb "to haul"* —*hauling as on a towpath* [les chemins de halage]—*very close to the hauling of the subject, who always drags his thing into a certain path that he cannot get out of . . .*

What we miss in the translation is only a small thing— the sense of *les chemins de halage,* yes, a towpath, in France, a path along a canal, perhaps lined by laurels, where a team of horses draw the barges along. What is missed in the phrase is the sense of compulsion, of duress, of *zwang* that the horses are subject to, and that the phrase carries within it. I can't help it. I am forced to haul this corpse along, driven by a whip if I stop to rest, even for a moment.

Why drag this corpse into the road, only to be smashed flat by the oncoming truck? Why so surprised each time?

No, those are the wrong questions—these are the
questions:

Can you put the corpse down?
Can you let the bag of rats drown?

James asked me why I didn't write poetry anymore. I have to go into a dark place inside myself to get that stuff, and without my father to pull me back out, I'm afraid to go in there anymore. Who will pull me out if I am lost?

I have to do this to keep you with me.

If I let you go I can stop.

This is why Freud calls it *Wiederholungszwang* [repetition compulsion]—and not just *Wiederholung* [repetition]. Because it is compulsory—one performs the repetition under duress—driven like an animal until you collapse in exhaustion and despair.

Aristotle described memory as a delayed motion that continues to exist in the soul, and repetition is a delayed motion *of* the soul, a motion in which the soul halts, stumbles, as it is running forward. Its force gathers as a wave behind you, to fall upon you, and in this motion— grief is returned to you.

There is a delay in the soul moving forward, a stumble, a hesitation. Say, for example, that the soul is a water moving forward in time, or that it is time itself, which falters in its forward momentum. The force of water delayed builds up behind it, and flips over into a wave. A delay, a falter, then a turning over: this is the motion. It is the force of the wave held back, the momentum of the motion delayed—that knocks you flat.

All this delay continues to exist in my soul.

[I am thinking of a great bubble—the kind made by children waving a wand—which rolls forward on the wind, wavers, folds over on itself, and breaks.

What soul are you thinking of?]

I was listening to a song you sent me today. *I'm going to make it through this year if it kills me.* I would repeat this refrain to myself, in the beginning, as I clawed my way back into New York like an animal.

I remember walking at night through the snow to the Bed-Stuy YMCA, scraped raw and crying. In the quiet, I heard my father's voice say, *You can do this.* What, I asked? *All of it.*

The people there were kind to me. The janitor would smile and say, Hello, Miss Rebecca!

This was the beginning honest feeling: I was dying when you met me. I could not get home.

You wrote me poems and explained Kant to me. You were honest and kind and sober.

To know that you were out there, wondering where I was—that you thought of me and smiled. It was a lot.

You were my one thread to the real world.

You woke me up.

Ramsey asked me what it was like. It was like being dead, I said, starting to cry—he teared up too—No—I touched his arm—it was nice. It's just coming alive again that is so horribly painful.

I know it's my fault, my father said to me, speaking of
my sister. He looked so broken. I told him it wasn't his
fault to make him feel better—also because I thought it
was my mother's fault.

This was the repetition: one knocks you down; the other
picks you up. By one you are struck down by the other
lifted up. Then the repetition can begin again.

It brought us to our knees and then we got up again.

This is the delayed motion,

in which you are so broken,

you can't get away.

This is the repetition.

He just got tired of catching us as we fell. It's ok, is the last thing I said to him before they closed the casket—I put my hands on his face, one on each cheek—It's enough—you can go now.

In the middle of the journey of our life, wrote Dante, I came to myself within a dark wood where the straight way was lost. I came to myself. I awoke and I was lost, I am lost still. The straight way was lost, and I have come, by this circuitous route, toward myself. I came to myself.

I am not victorious, I relinquish, I relinquish.

Consider a final verse from a poem by Celan:

Alles,
das Schwerste noch, war
flügge, nichts
hielt zurück.

All things,
even the heaviest, were
fledged, nothing
held back.

I could only guess at this, but I imagine that this honesty,
to hold nothing back, is love.

This is the repetition—I could see you through all of
this—I just could not get through it to reach you. I had
to write, as though under a terrible spell, until I arrived
in the present. I was running to get here.

It's not why I loved you—
only why I lost you.

I am deeply grateful to Martha Rhodes and Ryan Murphy (kind steward).

Thank you most of all to Wayne Koestenbaum, Kristin McTigue, Maggie Nelson, Ramsey Scott, and Susan Wheeler, for courage.

Thank you to my friends (Team France): Danièle Gibrat, Bruno Girodon, Arnaud Hédin, and Emmanuel Guy, for translation and artistic support, and to Charles Gute and Sally Ball, for editorial advice.

Special thanks to Bertrand Badiou and Eric Celan for the honor of permission to use the artwork of Gisèle Celan-Lestrange on the cover.

Rebecca Reilly teaches at The New School in New York. She has taught at Parsons, Paris, and The University of Paris, Nanterre. She is writing a dissertation on repetition in the work of Gertrude Stein at The Graduate Center of The City University of New York.

Publication of this book was made possible by grants and donations. We are also grateful to those individuals who participated in our 2014 Build a Book Program. They are:

Nickie Albert
Michele Albright
Whitney Armstrong
Jan Bender-Zanoni
Juanita Brunk
Ryan George
Michelle Gillett
Elizabeth Green
Dr. Lauri Grossman
Martin Haugh
Nathaniel Hutner
Lee Jenkins
Ryan Johnson
Joy Katz
Neal Kawesch
Brett Fletcher Lauer & Gretchen Scott
David Lee
Daniel Levin
Howard Levy
Owen Lewis
Paul Lisicky
Maija Makinen
Aubrie Marrin
Malia Mason
Catherine McArthur
Nathan McClain
Michael Morse
Chessy Normile
Rebecca Okrent
Eileen Pollack

Barbara Preminger
Kevin Prufer
Soraya Shalforoosh
Alice St. Claire-Long
Megan Staffel
Marjorie & Lew Tesser
Boris Thomas
William Wenthe